Managing the Complexities of Real Estate Development

T0291526

Managing the Complexities of Real Estate Development provides a concise summary of the real estate development process, allowing the reader to learn the fundamentals and details of development outside of the sink-or-swim environment of a particular project.

It offers early and mid-career real estate, legal, and financial professionals a behind the scenes view of the dynamic real estate development world, including: how developers make money, how development companies are structured, site location and acquisition, financial analysis, the design and development process, securing financing, project performance evaluation, and project sale or refinance. While focusing on multifamily apartment developments, the idiosyncrasies of retail, office, hotels, and mixed-use projects are also covered.

Robert H. (Bob) Voelker is a CPA, tax attorney, real estate attorney and multifamily developer with over 40 years' experience. He has a background in complex urban mixed-use, high-rise residential, and affordable housing development projects, as well as real estate finance, including institutional debt equity and creative financing alternatives. As part of the Senior Management Team at StreetLights Residential in Dallas, TX, he helped guide company strategy for high-rise and mixed-used development projects from inception through completion.

Managing the Complexities of Real Estate Development

Robert H. Voelker

Routledge
Taylor & Francis Group

NEW YORK AND LONDON

Cover image: HKS Architects

First published 2022
by Routledge
605 Third Avenue, New York, NY 10158

and by Routledge
4 Park Square, Milton Park, Abingdon, Oxon, OX14 4RN

Routledge is an imprint of the Taylor & Francis Group, an informa business

© 2022 Robert H. Voelker

Library of Congress Cataloging-in-Publication Data
Names: Voelker, Robert H., author.
Title: Managing the complexities of real estate development /
    Robert H. Voelker.
Description: New York, NY : Routledge, 2022. | Includes bibliographical
    references and index.
Identifiers: LCCN 2021053502 | ISBN 9781032206370 (paperback) |
    ISBN 9781032206387 (hardback) | ISBN 9781003264514 (ebook)
Subjects: LCSH: Real estate development. | Real estate
    development—Finance.
Classification: LCC HD1390 .V64 2022 | DDC 333.73/15—
    dc23/eng/20211222
LC record available at https://lccn.loc.gov/2021053502

ISBN: 978-1-032-20638-7 (hbk)
ISBN: 978-1-032-20637-0 (pbk)
ISBN: 978-1-003-26451-4 (ebk)

DOI: 10.1201/9781003264514

Typeset in Goudy
by Apex CoVantage, LLC

Contents

Figures

Acknowledgments

I am deeply thankful to my mentors – partners at my law firm who have been at the same time teachers, colleagues and friends throughout my career; real estate clients who allowed me a window into the development world; and the various developers who let me see behind the curtain and participate in the crafting of not just beautiful buildings, but fantastic places.

Foreword

Seasoned development professionals are prone to say that "every deal is complicated because all of the easy deals have been done", although much of the complexity is driven by the intricacies of our modern urban world and the level of diligence now required by 21st century financiers. In the pages that follow I unravel the complexities of real estate development, break down the concepts and the components into manageable bites, and offer the opportunity to advance years of knowledge in a short yet intense study for those who are new to the industry or just want to increase the breadth of their comprehension. Developers are by nature poor mentors, and navigating the development process without guidance while immersed in project deadlines can be daunting.

The goal of this book is to provide young developers, attorneys and debt and equity associates a giant leap forward in their careers by securing an in-depth behind the scenes view of the dynamic real estate development world, including how developers make money and how development companies are structured, locating and contracting to purchase a project location, financial analysis, the design and development process, securing project financing and ultimately refinancing or selling the project.

1 Introduction

In one of the first real estate development accounts in history,[1] the Babylonians attempted to create a magnificent city with a tower reaching to the heavens. God disrupted their plans by so confusing the languages of the workers that they could no longer understand each other. The city and the Tower of Babel were never completed. The story teaches an important lesson about unity, working together among diverse groups of people, the role of complexity in creating confusion and the sin of excessive pride. Thinking you know and can overcome everything oftentimes leads to one's downfall.

For its time, the Tower of Babel was a large edifice—a complex, abstract and imposing building. Frankly, there are very few real estate development projects today that are not abstract, imposing and complex. The purpose of this book is to unravel the complexities, to break down the concepts and the components into manageable bites, and to offer the opportunity to advance years of knowledge in a short yet intense study for those who are new to the industry or just want to increase the breadth of their comprehension.

The Tower of Babel story could easily be set in modern times—with land brokers, development associates, development companies, real estate attorneys, title companies, surveyors, consultants, lenders and equity partners—real estate development, from concept to architecture, development to construction, finance and sale is a massive endeavor with multiple parties, complexity and confusion. At times, particularly to those new to the process, it feels like you've been thrown into foreign waters and told to "swim," while simultaneously attempting to learn a foreign language. Developers are well known for their hubris, but they can be prone to holding their cards close to their vests and are by nature poor mentors. A large mixed-use project exists in five dimensions—the three dimensions of space with the added dimensions of time and chaos, and navigating the development process without guidance while facing impending project deadlines can be daunting.

In contrast, an organized and planned-out development pursuit can resemble a well-practiced three-ring circus, where the ringmaster brings together and

DOI: 10.1201/9781003264514-1

Figure 1.1 Tower of Babel by Peter Bruegel

orchestrates talented trainers, animals and entertainers from various parts of the world, all engaged in different acts and stunts to the same tune and with choreographed timing, earning applause for a great performance and bearing criticism for the entire troupe if the show fails. In overseeing the performers, the ringmaster must be organized, level-headed, diligent and persistent while constantly problem solving. The duties and physical requirements of a ringmaster are amazingly similar to those required of the lead developer or attorney for a complex real estate development. One commentator flippantly describes the job of a ringmaster as:

Duties:

- Managing the behavior of all circus performers and animal talent.
- Cleaning up after all animal talent and the smallest of the performers.
- Managing all daily appointments for performers and animals.
- Able to communicate with animals as well as performers and interpret their needs despite language barriers.
- Holding circus meetings to communicate when performance expectations are not being met. May require professional intervention.
- Providing training for animal talent.

Physical requirements:

- Must wear hearing protection. Subjected to whining, barking, yelling, meowing and crying on a daily basis.
- Must wear body armor. Animal talent known to claw, scratch and bark. May be required to break up altercations between animals and the small circus performers.
- Must be able to withstand the large amounts of alcohol it takes to manage all circus performers and animal talent. (Periodic liver scans required).[2]

Experienced real estate developers have learned the art of being an experienced ringmaster—managing the behavior of diverse personalities on the project team, including landowners, co-developers, architects, engineers and other design professionals, lenders, equity partners and their legal counsel, and setting up and managing all team appointments.

When one part of the team is underperforming, the developer must be willing to have the hard conversations about the need for every participant to meet expectations so that the entire project stays on time and on budget, with the required quality of output. A by-product of any major project is a lot of yelling and whining, and part of the developer's role is diplomatically presiding over stress and conflict. And in the midst of supervising the chaos, the lead developer must remain calm, directing the parties to the end goal. In the midst of the chaos, the developer should not forget to take care of himself/herself and his/her family members.

Due in large part to the substantial debt leverage used to finance real estate development, being a developer is a high risk/high reward endeavor. Development is a vocation largely learned through apprenticeship—on the job training, hopefully with a mentor, gaining experience and knowledge by mimicking the practices of others and through "lessons learned" from extraordinarily costly errors. Real estate developers take high stakes gambles on their projects, with substantial investments of their time, focus, energies and money, alongside funding from general and limited partner equity providers and lenders, with risky financial and performance guarantees provided by developer principals. Even the least complicated developments require long-term coordination of over a dozen different professionals focused on hundreds of practical, administrative, financial and legal details, all of which have to be investigated and managed in real time, an over-stimulating experience akin to juggling knives and chainsaws while running along a changing landscape, with a constant stream of new and challenging objects and obstacles being periodically lobbed into the mix from every angle. Moving development projects from finding a site to construction is, by necessity, a function of understanding complex processes, orchestrating the parties and attending to the details, making critical decisions in real time along the way.

As a tax lawyer who morphed into a real estate attorney; affordable housing attorney and then affordable housing developer; and then an urban mixed-use attorney who moved over to high-rise multifamily and mixed-use development, understanding processes and crafting and managing detailed checklists has been part of my career for 40 years. Real estate development is one of the most dynamic professions, involving at the same time both entrepreneurial and administrative skills, and crossing the boundaries of local politics, contract law, construction, finance and management. Participants in this field need a broad understanding in each of these disciplines. This treatise sets out a complete yet practical guide to the entire real estate development process as a useful training tool for students, developers, equity partners and lenders. Although the discussion centers largely around multifamily and mixed-use development, the principles discussed are equally applicable to all development projects, and later sections have been included that govern other types of development projects—hotels, office buildings, seniors' housing and retail projects.

This book is dedicated to young developers, attorneys and debt and equity associates of the future. There are facets of the development business that developers live with every day, and that attorneys and finance professionals need to understand to be able to properly craft transactions and draft better documents that reflect the realities of development instead of relying on rote provisions passed down from deal to deal. Similarly, there are aspects of real estate documents and structures that attorneys work with in all their agreements, but that most developers tend not to read and yet are critical components of interacting with design professionals, contractors, and debt and equity finance providers.

Much of the discussion that follows is deep and intricate, and oftentimes can only be fully understood while working through the challenges of developing an actual project. Where helpful I have included simple document provisions and organization charts, so that you can examine the individual concepts in context with the overall transaction. At the end of this book, I also offer additional reading recommendations, a glossary of defined terms and an index as handy reference tools as you pursue a particular real estate development and come across an unfamiliar phrase or concept.

Notes

1 Genesis 11:1–9.
2 https://nelsonfamilycircus.wordpress.com/2011/07/13/ringmaster-job-description/

2 How Developers Make Money

Over a 2–5-year project gestation period, developers leverage their ingenuity and hard work, including their willingness to take measured risks by guaranteeing construction loans and completion deadlines, with other people's money (OPM) to earn fees and project profits from sale or refinancing that are proportionately larger than the developer's capital invested as a percentage of the total capital.

By way of example, let's assume a $10 million development, with the construction lender financing 65%. The developer and its equity partners then fund equity of 35%, or $3.5 million, with the developer funding 10%, or $350,000 and the limited partner equity investors (LPs) funding 90%, or $3,150,000. The developer's proforma indicates that the project will receive current cash flow after debt service of 6% per year ($600,000) starting at the beginning of year 3, and the project sells at the end of year 5 for $12,000,000. Finally, the developer agrees to an overly simplistic split of profits from the project as follows (referred to as the distribution "waterfall"): 90% to the LPs and 10% to the developer (GP) until the LPs receive a 9% simple interest preferred return on and of their equity, then 65% to the LPs and 35% to the developer (GP).

Cash distributions to the owners would be as follows:

Year	Total Pref Return Due	Pref Paid	Rmng Pref Due
1	To GP = $ 31,500 To LP = $283,500	$0 $0	To GP = $31,500 To LP = $283,500
2	To GP = $ 63,000 To LP = $567,000	$0 $0	To GP = $ 63,000 To LP = $567,000
3	To GP = $ 94,500 To LP = $850,500	$ 60,000 $540,000	To GP = $ 34,500 To LP = $310,500
4	To GP = $ 66,000 To LP = $594,000	$ 60,000 $540,000	To GP = $ 6,000 To LP = $54,000
5	To GP = $ 37,500 To LP = $337,500	90%/10% to 9% pref To GP = $ 37,500 To LP = $337,500 Then 65%/35% To GP = $78,750 To LP = $146,250	

DOI: 10.1201/9781003264514-2

Year	Total Pref Return Due	Pref Paid	Rmng Pref Due
Sale	Proceeds – $12,000,000 – $6,500,000 mortgage payoff = $5,500,000	<u>Return Capital</u> To GP = $ 350,000 To LP = $3,150,000 <u>Balance 65%/35%</u> To GP = $ 700,000 To LP = $1,300,000	

In summary, the developer has received a total return on and of its capital of $1,286,250 on its $350,000 investment (or a 3.675 multiple), whereas the LP investors have received a total return of $6,013,750 on and of their capital $3,150,000 investment (or a 1.909 multiple). The developer receives an outsized return on its funds due to the developer having a share in profits that is greater than its capital contribution rate once the preferred return has been paid on invested capital. This excess return to the developer is referred to as the developer's "Promote."

In addition to earning the Promote, the developer will also typically earn a developer fee paid from the project equal to 3.5% to 4.0% of the total project cost excluding land and finance fees, and if the developer is also the contractor the developer would also be entitled to a contractor's fee. Finally, the LP partner may also allow the developer to earn an asset management fee upon project stabilization.[1]

Developers also look at their potential profit from sale of a project by referring to the "Cap Rate." The cap rate is determined by taking cash flow before debt service and dividing by the value of the property. Inversely, the value of the project is calculated by dividing the annual cash flow before debt service by the cap rate. For instance, a project yielding $100,000 of cash flow, valued in the market at a 5% cap rate, would be worth $20 million. A conservative developer will use a higher "build to cap rate" (the cap rate assumed when construction starts) and hope to achieve a lower exit cap rate (the cap rate on sale). In our example, if the cap rate on sale is 4.5%, the project with $100,000 in cash flow would now be worth over $22 million. In the best of all worlds, the developer would have forecasted conservative rents and expenses, and actual operations higher actual cash flow. If we assume the actual cash flow is $125,000 and the cap rate has dropped to 4.5%, the property could be sold for close to $28 million. Simply stated, the developer's and investors' goal is to have property operations outperform the proforma and to sell the project at a time when stabilized property investors are willing to pay a higher multiple on earnings to acquire the project.

Note

1 Additional reading: *How Real Estate Developers Think: Design, Profits and Community* by Peter Hendee Brown.

3 Development Company Structure

A thorough grounding in the structure of the typical development company is a precursor to comprehending a development project. Real estate entity organizational structure is largely a creature of legal and financial concerns over isolating entities and risk. Early in their careers, every young developer and real estate attorney should learn the art of drawing organizational and transactional charts, as understanding the relationships and interactions between the parties is absolutely critical to a firm grasp on the development process.

Typically a real estate developer is structured as a parent holding company owned by the developer principals, with (i) an underlying development holding company that has subsidiary, project-by-project development companies that serve as the developers for the individual projects (and earn development fees), and (ii) an underlying real estate ownership holding company that has subsidiary, project-by-project ownership companies (the "Developer GP Companies") that hold the developer's ownership stakes in the individual projects (in exchange for developer equity contributions and "sweat equity"). An additional entity may be added directly under the parent holding company to act as the contracting party under letters of intent and purchase contacts to isolate liabilities arising under those agreements from both the development fee income stream and the value of the assets under development and ownership. For each individual project, a Developer GP Company acts as the general partner (if the Project Owner is a limited partnership) or managing member (if the Project Owner is a limited liability company) that enters into a joint venture (the "Project Owner") with an institutional equity partner (the "LP Partner") who provides the remaining equity for the project. The remainder of the project capital is borrowed from a construction lender. The structure is illustrated in Figure 3.1.

During the course of development, a large number of agreements must be executed by the acquisitions and development entities, creating substantial monetary and legal obligations. Normally, to facilitate internal accounting controls only officers at a vice president or higher level will be authorized to sign these agreements, although development associates who are not officers

DOI: 10.1201/9781003264514-3

Figure 3.1 Organizational Chart 3.1 Simple Development Organizational Chart

are often permitted to execute purchase orders and professional service agreements below $5,000 or $10,000.

In the chapter on Project Financing, we will examine equity financing alternatives, and the development organizational structure chart will add additional layers.

4 Finding a Site

As the saying goes, real estate is all about "location, location, location," although that axiom is really a shorthand for the required level of investigation to determine a suitable site for a particular project. Strategically locating a successful real estate project is dependent on three inquiries: demographics, market research and local politics.

Demographics and Market Research

If you build a high-end retail center in an area where the incomes are not sufficient to support stores selling $250 pairs of jeans and $1,000 purses, retail purveyors (many of whom are national and international luxury goods conglomerates) will not lease space in that center. Similarly, if you develop a canned-goods-in-boxes grocery store in a higher income neighborhood, that store is unlikely to survive as the residents will be more inclined to shop at Whole Foods, Central Market or Trader Joe's. In the multifamily world, apartment complexes renting for $3.50 per square foot and those renting for $1.75 per square foot should, in the absence of subsidies to support lower rents, be located in entirely different neighborhoods. Detailed demographic research should be the starting point of a real estate development, and not an unsolicited email from a land broker offering up random available sites.

Developers are prone to skip the research phase, become enthralled with a new site before doing the research, and expend a great deal of time and money entering into a letter of intent, engaging an attorney to draft and negotiate a contract, reviewing survey and title, paying for environmental assessments and geotechnical studies, drawing up site plans, etc.—only to determine later that the proposed apartment complex will fail due to prevailing rents that won't support the project or too many similar projects are already planned or under construction in the submarket. And once a developer has invested significant funds and emotional energy in pursuing a site, a justification mentality can set in where key variables are pushed to make the project viable—"we can get higher rents than the competition because . . ." or "this site is special because . . ." or "we can add more units to lower our per unit costs and my proforma will then work . . ." The dreamed-of ends justify the means. Clarity of direction is much easier viewed from outside

DOI: 10.1201/9781003264514-4

the forest when you are not buried in the midst of the trees. Seasoned developers become students of sociology and demographics to grasp future trends in real estate demand.

> **Developers can easily become deal junkies—chasing deal after deal without any real evidence to support their vision. Invest in research first.**

Let's assume we want to develop a Dallas–Fort Worth (DFW) area apartment project. DFW continues to have a huge influx of new businesses and business expansions that drive growth, resulting in a fairly consistent need for new apartment development. But if the company that has just hired you as a young multifamily development associate wants to build a new project, where do you start?

- What quality of project is proposed, and what amenities will be offered? We often use a quick reference similar to Michelin star ratings for restaurants—should this be a five-star high-rise, highly amenitized project or a one-star garden apartment surface parked apartment project?
- Is your project targeting a particular demographic? Young professionals in studios and one-bedroom units? Active adults who desire larger units (and plenty of storage)?
- Given the project rating and target demographic, and what we know about operating expenses for that quality of project, what rents will be needed?
- Based on the answers to the first three questions above, what areas of DFW are securing those rent levels? And do those areas have the right age and income demographics?
- Within those areas, how many existing units are renting at that rate? Is the market "deep" or "shallow"? Are the projects all fairly new, have they rented up (been absorbed) quickly or taken a long time to rent? How many competing apartment projects are under construction or proposed?

Refining the proposed project as aimed at active empty nester adults with higher income levels helps to focus our research, beginning with finding the areas of town with overlapping high percentages of seniors, high household income levels and high house values. With a couple of days' census research, it is fairly easy to narrow down those areas of DFW where all three of these criteria overlap. Instead of waiting for a broker to send a site, and then sifting through the listings, attempting to separate the wheat from the chaff without any real guidance other than gut instinct, prospects for finding a site that will actually support the proposed development have dramatically improved. The target area should be determined before looking for sites. This same approach—using demographic research to refine target submarkets, can be applied to other forms of residential rental product, as well as retail, restaurant and office developments.

Overall, collecting and critically evaluating market research on construction costs, rents, absorption timing for new units (how quickly they will be rented after completion and start generating income), operating expenses and proposed competing developments in the same submarket help to avoid the "build it and they will come" trap which can lead to poor or even disastrous financial outcomes.

Local Political Will/Pressure

Homeowners become very vested in and highly protective of the status quo. Their two most important focal points are the value of their homes, one of their most significant assets, and the safety and education of their children. Local politicians and planning officials learn that their reelection prospects are largely dependent on supporting these agendas. Even if the proposed project is to be developed on land zoned for the intended use, local officials have a number of political, bureaucratic and administrative means at their disposal to hamper or delay a project that is opposed by area homeowners, such as refusing to approve plats or site plans or requiring impact fees, traffic studies and infrastructure enhancements.

A good broker can be a great resource and help you locate, evaluate and compare pieces of land. Before engaging a broker, explain in detail the type of project that is being proposed, the size of land tract required and the demographics needed for the project to be successful. Laying this preliminary foundation will put the developer and broker on the same wavelength up front, allowing the broker to present more relevant sites. A buyer's broker is normally paid by the seller through a commission split with the seller's broker, such that engaging a broker can expand the developer's site pursuits while not adding extra cost to the project.

Once a site is located and before contracting to purchase the property, an exploratory meeting with the city council person from the area and with the planning department will help uncover any bias against the proposed project, and they will likely require subsequent meetings with affected homeowner groups. Come prepared with renderings and a summary of how the project will benefit the community, and avoid being defensive.

> Twenty years ago, I proposed to develop an affordable housing apartment complex in a suburb of Dallas where I lived. The site was zoned multifamily at the density we wanted to build. Seemed like smooth sailing. We met with the planning department and they agreed it was appropriately zoned and we met with the mayor and various members of the city council, with the same result. Believing we could move forward, we applied for and were approved for low-income housing tax credit financing from the State of Texas. Three days after our financing was approved, the city denied our plat for the first time at a hearing where the homeowners were vehemently opposed to any low-income residents coming into the city, destroying their property values and putting apartment children into school with their children. The politicians backed the homeowners—to do otherwise would have been political

suicide—denied our plat four more times and then removed apartment zoning from the site. Three years later we settled our fair housing and state/federal takings claim against the city—but it would have been far more expedient to have met with local homeowner groups in advance to understand the political landscape. The effort on this one project took away time from multiple other potential projects, resulting in lost opportunities that could otherwise have been pursued.

Learn the local political hot buttons early, and if opposition is encountered, carefully evaluate whether to continue to pursue the project at that location, as each project pursuit uses the development company's most important resource—staff time, focus and emotional energy.

Although affordable housing is a particularly controversial development, planners and homeowners can also kill other types of unwanted projects by focusing on traffic concerns from retail, office or new, denser subdivisions; protecting the more "rural nature" of their city; impact on school capacity; etc.

5 Letters of Intent, Purchase Contracts, Ground Leases and Contribution Agreements

Once the appropriate submarket for the project is determined—based on demographics, market research and the political landscape—and a site has been located, discussions begin with the landowner to acquire the site. However, with prime sites in major metropolitan areas, it is not uncommon for a wealthy landowner to instead be focused on either long-term income from the site via a ground lease or by participating in a joint venture with the developer in order to share in the upside potential of investing in the development.

Letters of Intent

The first step toward acquiring a site is preparing a letter of intent (LOI)–sometimes called a term sheet)—which is typically done by the development partner or associate without involving outside legal counsel. Letters of intent typically provide that they are non-binding—they are merely a means to come to a basic understanding on the key terms of the acquisition, such as:

- Purchase price or value given to the land if contributed to the development.
- If land is contributed, the framework for how the landowner receives a return on invested land value.
- Earnest money—when is it refundable, and when does it become nonrefundable (referred to as "hard" earnest money). The developer should keep a detailed summary of all critical dates concerning earnest money and set up a calendar reminder system to track when earnest money deposits are required and when the funds become nonrefundable, so that the developer can determine comfort level with continuing to pursue the project versus terminating the contract and receiving the return of the earnest money.
- Due diligence/feasibility/inspection period (these terms are interchangeable).
- If applicable, time to rezone for the intended use or secure necessary development entitlements, and if the entitlements are not received, the earnest money is refundable to the developer/purchaser.
- Timing of closing with possible rights to extend with additional earnest money or extension payments.

DOI: 10.1201/9781003264514-5

- The process for closing the transaction.
- Miscellaneous provisions.

The letter of intent will not deal with all of the details that will ultimately be covered in the purchase and sale agreement, contribution agreement or option to ground lease; however, the LOI does set the framework for the relationship of the parties, and taking the time to carefully negotiate the LOI will reduce future areas of disagreement (which may otherwise only arise after considerable money has been expended on due diligence costs and legal fees).

Earnest Money

Because developers typically chase a number of sites, depositing a lot of earnest money for each site can add up quickly, dictating that developers negotiate for the smallest possible amount of earnest money amount. A number of factors play into the amount of earnest money that will be acceptable to the seller, including the purchase price, desirability of the location, difficulty in securing rezoning or entitlements and whether the seller is putting the site out to market broadly or privately. As a very rough guide, initial earnest money for a site that is not widely marketed might be in the following ranges:

Purchase Price	Initial Earnest Money
$5–10 million	$100,000–250,000
$10–25 million	$200,000–350,000

At least until after the end of the due diligence period, earnest money is typically refundable (i.e., the developer has a "free look" during the due diligence period). A smaller amount of earnest money may be feasible during the due diligence period, with additional earnest money (frequently equal to or greater than the initial earnest money set forth above) being deposited upon the expiration of the due diligence period.

> *If the developer does not terminate the contract by the end of the feasibility period the earnest money goes hard and is nonrefundable to the developer unless other contingencies are stated in the contract that require the return of the earnest money.*

Title/Survey Review Period

In most cities, a title commitment and survey can be obtained in 30–45 days. An additional 10 business days after the receipt of the last of the title commitment and survey should be allowed for the developer's legal counsel to review and provide formal comments, in a "title/survey objection letter," informing the seller, the title company and the surveyor of unacceptable aspects of the title and survey. The seller will then have a shorter period, typically 7–10 business days, to respond in writing to the objections, by agreeing to either remedy the objections prior to closing or refusing to address the problems, in which case the buyer can either terminate the purchase contract (and receive the return of its earnest money) or agree to accept title with the objectionable item. The surveyor and title company may also indicate which items they are willing to delete or revise; however, title companies are governed by state laws that may restrict how various title exceptions can be modified, and certain modifications require the payment of additional title endorsement fees.

Title commitments indicate who is the current owner of the property, exceptions to title that could potentially remain with the property if not cleared up and removed, title encumbrances that will remain but must be complied with or further investigated, and exceptions that the seller will be expected to remove (although the seller may still refuse to do so). A survey should be delivered to the title company prior to the title commitment being issued, so that the title company can review the survey for any additional "on the ground" encroachments onto or from adjacent properties, as well as structures or facilities on the site that may not be within recorded easements (e.g., utility boxes or poles). The title company uses the survey to add additional title exceptions arising from the survey.

> *In preparing the title objection letter, the developer and developer's counsel should closely examine each title exception and the survey for any matters that could affect the potential development.*

Careful attention should be paid to easements running through the property, such as utility easements, access rights, etc. as relocating underground or above-ground utilities or securing revisions to or removal of access rights can be costly and time-consuming. For instance, in a recent review of survey and title on a property in Fort Worth we noticed that there was an old abandoned alley down the center of the property, and under that alley was a sewer easement that was not abandoned and apparently served not only the site but the properties across streets to the north and south of the property, making our proposed apartment complex impossible without relocating this trunk utility line. Title and survey review requires a highly critical examination of every small detail and is best learned sitting beside a paralegal or attorney who has years of experience.

Any title exceptions that will remain may need further investigation. For instance, if there are covenants, conditions and restrictions (CCRs) or owner association documents on title, those documents should be reviewed to determine if there are any delinquent dues (which may carry over to the new owner), any restrictions on what can be built on the site (which may be in addition to zoning requirements), whether certain building materials are required or prohibited, and whether an owner's association or design review board must approve the plans for the proposed development. An estoppel letter should be obtained from the applicable party to address any open CCR or owner association issues.

See the footnote for additional resources on survey/title objection letters.[1]

Due Diligence Period

As discussed in more detail in the next section, site due diligence involves third party investigations and reports, which take time to secure, review and determine appropriate action. The buyer/developer should ask for at least 90–120 days to research site conditions and, to address problems that may arise, extension rights should be secured if possible; for example, two 30-day extensions by depositing additional earnest money of $X per extension. This additional earnest money should also be nonrefundable until the end of the due diligence period; however, the seller may require that due diligence extension payments be nonrefundable. Whether extension payments are applicable to the purchase price is negotiable between the buyer and seller.

Rezoning/Entitlement Contingency

If the proposed site is not zoned for the intended use or if additional local entitlements are required to have a developable site (e.g., site plan approval, local architectural or property owner approval, securing a liquor license), an additional period of time should be allowed to secure such approvals. Determining the needed time period will require discussions with the party that grants the approvals, but it is not uncommon for a rezoning to take 9–12 months, and in some states like California full entitlement approvals may take longer than a year. During this period the earnest money is typically hard (i.e., no longer refundable) *except for* if the needed approvals are not secured. Options for extension should also be requested in exchange for additional earnest money, in the event that the approvals are delayed. Typically the purchase contract will require that the developer keep the seller informed of progress in securing the zoning or entitlements.

Closing Period

Most developers do not want to own sites until they have secured financing and building permits and are ready to start construction, as most lenders and equity partners are not willing to finance land acquisition and risk owing the property without knowing if all financing will ultimately be available or if construction costs will make the project unprofitable. Even if a land loan can be secured, it will typically require 50% or more equity and/or a guarantee from a credit worthy entity. With the time required for site due diligence, possible rezoning/entitlements, preparation of plans, securing site plan approvals, building permits and debt and equity financing, closings on development parcels typically occur 9–15 months after the purchase contract is signed. Extensions should be negotiated, but in this case extension earnest money is often non-refundable (other than for seller default) and not applicable to the purchase price.

Sites with Existing Tenants

Occasionally the chosen site contains buildings with existing tenants. The seller will be reluctant to terminate leases and lose tenant lease payments prior to closing the sale of the property, whereas the developer will want to start construction immediately after the closing so as to not hold land for an extended period of time. If the leases terminate prior to the closing, once earnest money is hard on the purchase contract the seller may be willing to work with the tenants on month-to-month leases until shortly before closing, providing the tenants 60–90 days' notice of the closing date. In this case, if the developer then extends the closing date, the tenants will have vacated, so typically the seller will ask the purchasing developer to make up the lost revenue through closing. If one or more leases extend past the closing, during the feasibility period the seller and developer will need to negotiate a buy-out of the tenant's lease, and the letter of intent should address which party pays this expense. If the lease termination is not ultimately secured, the developer should have the right to the return of the earnest money.

Miscellaneous LOI Provisions

Standard additional provisions in an LOI include (i) brokerage commission and whether seller or buyer pays the commission; (ii) an exclusive period where the seller will remove the property from the market and not entertain any additional offers while the purchase and sale agreement is being negotiated; and (iii) confidentiality of the LOI terms.

> **Most importantly,** *the letter of intent should conclude with a paragraph that clearly indicates that it is nonbinding (except for confidentiality, exclusivity and removal from market) and that a contract between the parties does not exist until the "definitive document" (the purchase and sale agreement, contribution agreement or option to ground lease) is fully executed.*

Contribution Agreements

When land is held by a seller who is not motivated by an immediate cash sale, particularly in urban environments, and the landowner is comfortable with development risk, the transaction may be proposed as a contribution to and investment by the landowner in the project, which will require revisions to the letter of intent.

With land contributions, the value of the land, similar to a purchase price, should be agreed to in the LOI, or alternatively the land could be appraised during the early part of the inspection period and the parties could then either agree to this value or terminate the LOI. This deemed value then becomes a contribution to the general partner entity (a joint venture between the developer and the landowner), even though the land is actually directly contributed to the owner venture that includes the limited partner investor that provides the majority of the capital for the project. The landowner's deemed contribution value to the GP entity then earns either a general partner level return (which includes a portion of the developer "promote" and possibly a portion of the developer fees) or, more likely, a limited partner level return that does not share in the promote or developer fees. "Promote" means the portion of the cash flow paid by the project owner to the developer (or the joint venture between the developer and a co-GP partner, as described below) that is disproportionate to the capital contributions made by the developer to the project owner. Visually, the transaction would appear as follow:

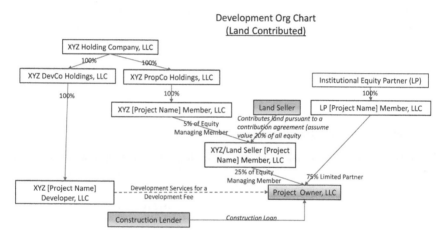

Figure 5.1 Organizational Chart 5.1 – Development Organizational Chart (Land Contributed)

In a land contribution scenario, the return to the landowner could be described in the letter of intent as follows:

> Landowner will enter into a Contribution Agreement to contribute the Site to the Owner Venture at a value equal to $_____ and will receive a capital account credit in the Owner GP equal to such amount (the "**Land Value**"), being the agreed fair market value of the Site. The Owner GP will be a joint venture between an affiliate of the Developer, as the managing member/general partner, and the Landowner as the non-managing member/limited partner. The Owner Venture will be comprised of the following members (the "**Owner Members**"): the Owner GP as the general partner/managing member and an institutional capital partner as the limited partner/

non-managing member (the "**LP**"). Upon closing of the Owner Venture, Landowner will contribute the Site to the Owner Venture. The Landowner's rate of return on the Land Value will be the same rate of return earned by the LP in the Owner Venture joint venture agreement.

The landowner may desire to only contribute a portion of the land value such that the land transaction is a partial sale (for cash at the closing) and a contribution. Typically upon execution of the contribution agreement construction costs, loan interest rates, limited partner equity returns and other critical factors affecting the project financial performance are not yet determined, such that the landowner won't be in a position to definitively decide to make an entire or partial land contribution versus just selling the site. To address this concern, the letter of intent may allow time for the developer to flesh out the project pro-forma and the limited partner investment terms, and for the landowner to then opt to sell or contribute; however, this determination by the landowner should be required months in advance of closing as the investment by the landowner impacts on the amount of equity required from and the terms of the investment with the institutional equity partner creates additional complexity in the deal organizational structure (i.e., the joint venture agreement between the developer and the landowner) and may alter certain terms with the construction lender.

If the amount of deemed land equity contributed by the landowner is substantial in relation to the total equity required for the project, or if the landowner also agrees to provide additional cash equity to raise its stake in the project, the landowner may negotiate for approval rights over major decisions affecting the project, similar to the rights held by the institutional limited partner equity. In general the developer should resist this request unless the landowner is contributing the entire amount of non-developer project equity, as conflicts will then arise between the approval rights of the landowner and approval rights of the institutional equity partner, hampering both the ability to secure the entire project capital or creating contentious squabbles over which party's approval rights have priority. Any approval rights ceded to the landowner should be agreed to in the letter of intent.

If the landowner's land equity contribution is substantial, and the landowner is open to participating in development risk, the developer may also request that the landowner contribute toward predevelopment costs prior to the equity and debt closings and/or that the landowner contribute cash in addition to the value of the land. In this scenario, the developer may share a portion of the Promote with the landowner to compensate for the additional risk being assumed should the project not secure financing or otherwise not proceed. The sharing arrangement for predevelopment costs should also be set forth in the LOI with the landowner. If the landowner is contributing to the project beyond just the value of the land, the joint venture agreement with the landowner should contain remedy provisions dealing with failure of the landowner to contribute. Typical remedies include the developer making the landowner's capital contribution as a priority loan with a high interest rate or the developer making the defaulted contribution but treating that contribution as watering down the landowner's sharing ratio on a 1.5 or 2.0 times basis.

Options to Ground Lease

If a landowner is already wealthy, and is looking for long-term cash flow for the balance of his/her life and into future generations, or is adverse to development risk, a ground lease may be proposed. Ground leases of land to be developed come with a number of complications. The dynamics of the interrelationships of ground lessor, developer, equity partner and construction lender can resemble a dysfunctional family, where the smallest controversy can turn into a big battle, which largely explains why developments on ground leases are difficult to finance and close. In fact, many LP partners will not provide equity for projects on ground leases. In addition, many construction lenders require unencumbered title to the land underlying a construction project, and may require that the ground lease be subordinated to the lien of the construction loan, meaning that if the project goes into default the lender can eliminate the ground lease (and associated payments) to the property owner/ground lessor and take title to not only the improvements, but also to the underlying land. Very few landowners are willing to subordinate their ground leasehold interests and risk losing the value of the cash flow stream from the ground lease or the residual value of the land.

If the landowner insists on a ground lease structure, the letter of intent will be altered to provide for the basic terms of the ground lease, which generally speaking are as follows:

- **Option to ground lease**: instead of a purchase and sale agreement, the parties will enter into an option to ground lease, with the ground lease itself fully negotiated and attached, and if not attached, will be negotiated within a short period of time (suggestion: 90–120 days and before the end of the inspection period) after the option to ground lease is executed. The danger with a lengthy negotiation period is that ground leases are very detailed and subject to extensive dialogue between the landowner and the developer (with input from the LP equity partner), and failure to agree to terms could result in a significant amount of wasted due diligence time and expense (particularly sizable attorneys' fees).
- **Term** (including extensions): extending to at least 99 years.
- **Annual payments**: after construction completion, 4–6% of the value of the land (determined by appraisal). During construction the payments will be reduced to between $0 and 50% of the post-construction payment amount. Prior to signing the ground lease (which normally occurs upon closing of the construction loan and start of construction), smaller monthly payments may be required to offset the landowner's costs while the land is held under

contract. Typically the ground rent will reset every 5–10 years to the same percentage of a newly appraised "as if" value of the land (as it existed before the project was built), but with a cap on the amount of the increase, as otherwise the project would be unfinanceable given the uncertainty of such increases. Alternatively, the step up in rent could be tied to the increase in the consumer price index (CPI) for that region over the period from the inception of the ground lease to the date of the reset, but subject to a cap of X% per year.

- **Subordination and nondisturbance/attornment agreements**: As mentioned above, the ground lease is typically not subordinated, and this should be stated in the LOI. To protect the LP equity partner and the construction and future lenders, those parties enter into a "nondisturbance and attornment agreement" ("NDA") with the landowner, where the financing parties are given notice of a default under the ground lease and additional time to cure such default if not cured by the developer/ground lessee. Additionally, even if the default is not cured, additional time is given to the lender (or any purchaser at a foreclosure sale) post-foreclosure of its loan to enter into a new ground lease with the landowner, on substantially the same terms as the ground lease between the landowner and the developer. Oftentimes the actual form of the NDA is fully negotiated with and attached to the ground lease.
- **Closing date**: given the complexity of negotiating and financing ground leases, the timeline for closing is typically much longer than with a simple land purchase contract, and often the landowner agrees to just keep working with a developer who is diligently pursuing financing and is keeping the landowner informed of progress. In this respect the relationship of the parties takes on the characteristics of a development joint venture.

A typical structure chart for a ground lease transaction would be as follows:

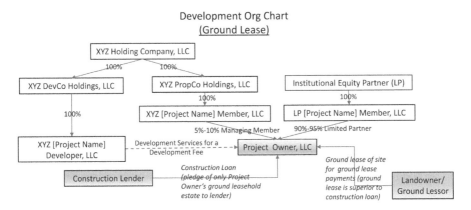

Figure 5.2 Organizational Chart 5.2 – Development Organizational Chart (Ground Lease)

Partial Land Contributions & Partial Ground Leases

Negotiations with landowners occasionally take on added complexity, such as partial sales and partial contributions of land, reduced ground lease payments with the landowner capitalizing a certain portion of the land value as a deemed contribution to the project or a full ground lease payment with the landowner agreeing to contribute cash to the project.

Joint Ventures and Cooperation Agreements for Mixed-Use Projects

Mixed-use projects with multiple developers working on various components require fluidity and attention to the soft science of long working relationships with multiple developers/owners. To set the backdrop, assume we are going to develop apartments, office space, a hotel and a restaurant. The parking garage for the office, hotel and restaurant are underground below the apartments, the restaurant and apartment lobby are on the ground floor of the apartments, with 4 floors of above-ground parking for the apartments and the apartment tower then sits above this podium. The restaurant, office, hotel and apartments will all be developed by and owned by different parties.

Among the many details to determine and cover in the letter of intent between the parties are:

- Who owns or will contract to purchase the site? How will the various owners share in earnest money and due diligence costs? How will land purchase contract decisions be made?
- Will the project have one architect or multiple architects? In our example, it is unlikely that a single architect will be well versed in all of these product types. If there are multiple architects, will one of the architects serve as the lead/coordinating architect and as the architectural control committee, setting design standards for a unified theme for the entire mixed-use project?
- The parking garage will need to be structured as a commercial condominium regime, so that the individual developers have ownership over their parking spaces. How will the parking garage construction, maintenance and management costs be allocated among the parties? Will parking spaces be shared between uses, and how does this affect the sharing ratio for costs?
- In the parking garage/restaurant/apartments tower, typical office parking spaces are wider than apartment parking spaces, resulting in differing support column spacing (note that if a grocery store were part of the product mix, column spacing becomes much wider as it is critical to in-store aisle accessibility). These differing column spacing grids will likely require an "interstitial floor" in the building to transfer the floor loads and utility connections from one grid to another, which creates a significant increase in project costs. How should these added costs be shared among the owners?

- How will common area costs such as internal roads, sidewalks, landscaping and public art be shared between the parties?
- Who will manage the owners' association and how will the board member votes be allocated among the owners?

> *On complex mixed-use projects, only partner with developers who show extreme creativity in addressing obstacles and flexibility in reaching compromises.*

The number of issues to address throughout design, construction and operation, the changing dynamics as details are considered, the hurdles that arise and the number of documents that must be negotiated with multiple parties (and their counsel) over many months will exert strain on even positive relationships, and having one or more difficult personalities in the mix will either aggravate the situation or torpedo the entire transaction. In addition, find legal counsel that has been battle tested in complex mixed-use projects, and when lawyer disagreements arise on business and legal points be prepared to intervene and "manage" your attorney by seeking direct agreement among the business parties (although separately seeking your attorney's advice on the risks involved in reaching a compromise position).

Developer Fees; Contractor Fees

Fees payable to the developer and its affiliates are typically mentioned in letters of intent if the landowner will ultimately be a part owner in the project, even though the ultimate determination of the amount and timing of these fees lies with the main equity partner (LP partner) and the construction lender. Developer fees typically range from 3–4.5% of total project costs (but excluding land cost and interest payments and other financing fees associated with the construction loan). Developer fee timing varies and must be negotiated with equity and debt providers, but often is phrased as "X% [*typically from 10% to 25%*] at loan closing/start of construction, Y% during the course of construction as a percentage of completion of the project, and the remaining Z% [*from 10% to 20%*] upon attaining the final certificate of occupancy for the project." Contractor fees are dependent on whether a third party contractor builds the project (possibly 3.5% of construction costs) or an affiliate of the developer is the contractor (ranging from 4% to 4.5% of construction costs). When a third party contractor is selected, the developer and contractor normally enter into a "guaranteed maximum price" construction contract, with this lower fee, which at first blush looks beneficial to the project equity partners; however, major third party contractors have a tendency to negotiate a lower fee and a lower construction bid to "win" the construction contract, but then carefully document every small change order, driving up the final cost of construction, whereas a developer-related contractor will have a greater tendency toward determining a more accurate final construction cost—given involvement in the project from the outset and given that the developer (and its related contractor) will ultimately be responsible to the lender and equity partners for all or a large share of any construction cost overruns.

Note

1 'A Walk through a Typical Objection Letter' by Charles Craig, www.stewart.com/content/dam/stewart/Microsites/texas/pdfs/2019/112119%20Slides.pdf; Title and Survey Objection Letters Guidelines and Solutions by G. Roland Love and Paul McNutt, Jr., www.texasbarcle.com/Materials/Events/10949/144475.pdf

6 Initial One-Pager Financial Analysis

During the period between finding a site and executing the letter of intent, the developer develops and analyzes a very rough financial proforma of the proposed project. With a historical understanding of construction costs for the chosen product type, and market research on rents for other projects in the areas (with due consideration for the age and quality of the pre-existing projects versus the proposed project) and operating costs for similar product, a rough proforma can be created to determine if the project is feasible. Absorption—how quickly after units are completed will they be rented and start generating income—is critical in sizing the construction loan interest reserve (one component of total project cost), as failure to provide for adequate lease-up time may result in the developer being forced to "feed" the project with additional equity to keep from defaulting on the construction loan.

At this point, the proforma is very preliminary, as market studies have not been ordered, architectural and engineering plans have not been prepared and actual construction costs have not been determined. Even if the preliminary proforma looks promising, the project economics at this stage are at best an educated guess and the project is not certain to proceed—the one-pager is merely a "gut check" on whether the developer should continue to pursue the project. Becoming enamored with the project at an early stage can impair the ability to apply critical financial analysis, necessitating the balancing act of being a "realistic optimist," pushing the envelope of opportunity but only taking calculated, informed risks. Seek (and actually listen to) those around you. To facilitate a healthy dialogue and analysis, assign one person to be the contrarian, to be the devil's advocate against each project.

The most profitable project you do may be the one you walk away from— the one that would lose tons of money because you were too much of a pioneer, or too locked into the site or the vision or just needed to do a project to fill the pipeline, to cover your overhead.

To borrow from a wild west analogy, being a cautious pioneer can be enthralling; being the scout that goes out in front of the wagon train can easily get you shot in the back with arrows.

DOI: 10.1201/9781003264514-6

At each stage of development, the developer should ask two tough questions:

(i) Is this project feasible—have I used valid, truly justifiable numbers for project costs and project revenue and expense?
(ii) Should I expend my most important resource—my time, focus and emotional energy—on this project or another project that has a greater probability of actually being constructed and of earning a high rate of return?

Project costs should be re-evaluated and anticipated project rents/selling prices should be updated at each critical juncture of project development, to determine if the project justifies the risk and still meets debt and equity financing metrics.

After the first draft of the proforma is created, alternatives are considered: can we lower costs or increase rents by selecting a different product type (e.g., garden style surface parked apartment complex vs. wrap project with structured parking), by adding or subtracting amenities and services, by increasing or reducing the number of units, etc. Until the project is within earshot of feasibility, pursuit costs should be closely monitored and kept to a minimum and purchase contract earnest money should not be allowed to "go hard" and become nonrefundable.

7 Keeping Tabs on Pursuit Costs, Avoiding "Dead Deal Costs" and Balancing the Pursuit Portfolio

As mentioned above, most development companies are constantly chasing multiple transactions—a medium-size developer could have 20–30 sites under review and another 10–15 active deal pursuits. The aggregate inspection and due diligence costs, including earnest money, could easily total in the millions of dollars. Given the complexities of development and the challenges of deal pursuits, one of the endearing qualities of most developers is their extreme optimism—fearlessly chasing difficult sites and complex projects, viewing the prospects through rose colored glasses, seeing the potential upside and minimizing (and sometimes ignoring) the downside risks.

If the property needs to be rezoned to permit the development, zoning attorneys and local political consultants may need to be hired to engage with city council members and homeowner/property owner associations. In multifamily development, rezoning (or seeking greater entitlements such as more height or higher floor-area-ratio) can result in the city requiring a percentage of affordable housing, which can dramatically affect the economics of the project, potentially making it infeasible.

Mixed-use projects that involve multiple uses, multiple developers and site aggregation are an adrenaline rush for developers—enticing, cool and sexy—and with all their allure they are like an extended dating relationship with a high maintenance, very volatile partner. The experience can be both invigorating and, over time, extremely tiring, with no certain end result. Mixed-use projects drastically increase the number of meetings and conference calls to coordinate schedules and integrate development plans and construction; typically have multiple developers, debt and equity partners (and legal counsel), all of which must come to terms on complex documents outlining the relationships of the parties; and oftentimes come with pre-leasing requirements (e.g., 50% of retail or 50% of office components need to be preleased) that must occur before the project can proceed, all while the parties are spending millions of pursuit dollars. Chasing one complex mixed-use project that requires 3–4 times the effort (and cost) comes at the expense of multiple single use projects that are easier to push through the development process. The most valuable and limited resource at a development

DOI: 10.1201/9781003264514-7

company is not money or even projects, but rather the time and energy of very talented people, and investing that resource wisely is critical to success.

> *The thoughtful development associate, who is frequently paid a portion of the profits from each project they pursue, will focus on balancing out his/her pursuit portfolio, with a smaller percentage of "home run" complex mixed-use pursuits or projects that require rezoning or entitlements and a larger percentage of "singles and doubles"—straightforward single use projects on zoned and entitled land.*

This balanced perspective will also limit exposure to unrecoverable costs if a pursuit fails to secure zoning or pre-leasing or if one of the developers in a mixed-use project is unable to secure financing.

8 Purchase and Sale Agreements, Contribution Agreements and Options to Ground Lease

A binding agreement between the landowner and the developer does not exist until the parties execute the definitive document—a purchase and sale agreement (PSA), land contribution agreement or option to enter into ground lease. In broad terms, the definitive document should follow the agreed to provisions in the letter of intent, but flesh out the details and cover standard business and legal terms based on the property locale.

Standard Contract Provisions

All contracts to acquire real property, in whatever form, have certain prototypical provisions that define the parties and their contractual obligations, such as the following.

Consideration

In most states, a contract is not binding unless there is consideration, something of value, that passes between the parties at the time the contract is signed, and refundable earnest money does not constitute consideration. Thus, a typical contract will provide at the outset "For and in consideration of Ten Dollars and other good and valuable consideration from buyer to seller, the receipt and sufficiency of which is hereby acknowledged . . ." In addition the contract should provide that if the purchaser terminates the contract, a small amount of the earnest money (e.g., $100) will, instead of being returned to the buyer, be distributed by the escrow holder to the seller as "independent consideration" for the option to acquire the property (or have the property contributed or ground leased, as the case may be) given by the seller to the purchaser during the feasibility period and up until closing.

Representations and Warranties/Covenants

The purchaser should ask for a number of standard representations and warranties from the seller, including (but not limited to) the following:

- **Authority**: seller has the authority to enter into the contract and entering into the contract does not violate any agreement binding on the seller.

DOI: 10.1201/9781003264514-8

- **Existence and good standing**: The seller entity is in existence and good standing in the state of its formation.
- **No occupancy rights or service agreements**: There are no leases or other licenses, concession agreements, occupancy agreements or service contracts binding on any portion of the property and there will be no such agreements at the closing, with a listing of any such agreements currently in place.
- **No condemnation**: To seller's knowledge, there are no pending actions to condemn (take for public use) any portion of the property.
- **No unpaid taxes**: Except for current year taxes (which will be prorated between the buyer and seller at closing), there are no property taxes or other taxes unpaid by seller that could constitute a lien on the property.
- **No violation of environmental or other laws**: Seller has not received written notice of any violation of environmental or other laws pertaining to the property.
- **No contracts to sell property to others**: Seller has not entered into a contract to sell the property to another buyer.
- **Not to enter into other agreements affecting the property**: Seller agrees not to enter into any agreements encumbering the property during the pendency of the purchase agreement without the written approval of the purchaser.

The contract should further state a survival period after closing for the seller's representations and warranties (normally from 6 months to a year).

Purchaser Contracting Party and Assignability

As stated above, most developers have a separate "acquisitions" entity that executes letters of intent and purchase and sale agreements. The purchase contract should specifically allow the acquisition entity to assign the contract, *without seller's approval*, to any entity controlled by the principals of the developer.

Notices

A notice provision should be added to the contract, laying out the notice parties (typically purchaser, seller, their legal counsel and the title company), the means by which written notices may be given, such as mail, overnight delivery and email, and whether notice from a party's counsel constitutes notice by that party.

Choice of Law and Venue

The parties should agree in the contract that the laws of the state where the property is located will be applied to any disputes and that any such disputes will be held in a particular county in that state (referred to in legal jargon as "venue" for the dispute).

Dispute Resolution

If a conflict should occur between the parties, a mechanism should be established for resolving the issue. Most purchase and sale contracts defer directly to litigation and do not utilize either nonbinding mediation or binding arbitration, although those options could be considered and may be preferable in the case of contribution agreements and options to ground lease, given the complexity of those structures and the need for the parties to not have one or more minor disputes upset the much larger transaction.

Remedies

To address the potential defaults in the parties' obligations, the contract should clearly set forth the remedies for the non-defaulting party. The seller's remedies should be *strictly limited* to confiscating the buyer's non-refundable earnest money. The buyer's remedies should include (i) terminating the contract and receiving the return of its earnest money and any extension payments deposited with the seller—and possibly receiving reimbursement of the buyer's out-of-pocket costs in pursuing the property, up to some capped amount, or (ii) specific performance of seller's obligations under the contract (i.e., conveying the property to the buyer). In addition, the non-defaulting party should have the ability to recover its reasonable attorneys' fees in pursuing their remedies.

Rollback Taxes

In some states a landowner who keeps the property in some form of agricultural or livestock use will have the land taxed at a much lower rate; however, conversion to another use will trigger a "rollback" tax that is owed calculated at the higher non-agricultural rate for a certain number of years (e.g., 3–5 years) prior to the change in use. The amount of this rollback can be significant, and the purchase contract should state whether the seller or buyer is responsible for the rollback tax payment. If the developer/buyer is paying the rollback taxes, the developer should make certain that this increased cost of acquiring the land is included in project costs.

Tracking Contract Deadlines

If key contract deadlines pass unnoticed, the buyer/developer's earnest money could be lost or the seller may have the right to terminate the contract, wasting months of work and causing dead deal pursuit cost losses. Once the contract has been executed, one of the most critical tasks for the developer is tracking critical deadlines. This task is best begun by reviewing the contract with a highlighter, and then making a list of due dates for earnest money delivery, title and survey delivery and objections, rezoning or site plan delivery to the seller, etc. Calendar reminders should then be established several days in advance of each due date, with at least two development company staff members and outside counsel copied on the reminders.

Site Due Diligence

In addition to reviewing survey and title, several site evaluations should be commissioned to make certain the site does not have adverse conditions that could affect buildability or the cost of construction, as follows:

- **Topographical survey**: The surveyor should be commissioned to prepare a survey showing the existing topography of the site, including any creeks, streams or escarpments. The development site plan should take these conditions into account, and costs for grading or soil import and any needed bridges to traverse waterways should be determined and added to total projects costs in the proforma.
- **Geotechnical soils report**: These reports are typically performed by an engineering firm, and evaluate the water table level and plasticity or movement of the soil and potential water table to determine how the foundations need to be designed and constructed. If the soil has a heavy clay content, lime treatment or injection may be required to stabilize the site, or additional steel, thicker concrete or deeper footings may be required in the foundation. If the water table lies within the depth of the concrete footings, the site may need to be dewatered or different construction techniques may be required for subsurface concrete footings or garages, all of which will drive up the cost of the project.
- **Environmental reports**: Once the site is under contract, an environmental consulting firm should be engaged to perform a Phase I environmental study, doing a visual assessment of the site and researching the history of the property and surrounding sites to determine if there have been any prior uses or readily apparent environmental concerns that could create hazards for the potential development and its users. Prior uses that give grounds for additional inquiry are: dry cleaning plants; gas stations or oil tanks, whether above ground or below ground; chemical manufacturing plants; the presence of asbestos or lead based paint in existing buildings on the site; etc. These reports typically start with an executive summary of their findings where concerns are noted, but the entire report should be reviewed to identify potential (costly) actions that may be needed to clean up the site. If the consulting firm notes areas of further inquiry, a Phase II investigation may be in order, which may involve subsurface drilling or "destructive testing" for asbestos in walls, flooring mastic or around pipes. In additional to hazardous materials on the site, the environmental report should also indicate if the site contains ponds or other protected wetlands, which may trigger the need for a determination of whether the developer can either alter the site plan to work around any such areas or, alternatively, seek governmental approvals

to remove the wetlands areas by creating additional wetlands in the immediate area. Environmental concerns can be very technical (i.e., understanding permitted amounts of toxic substances based on proposed use), and unless a thorough review of the environmental report is done by an environmental attorney, the developer/buyer as successor owner of the property can potentially be held liable for previously existing environmental conditions that are not properly addressed.

- **Flood plain**: The site survey should indicate whether any portions of the site lie within a flood hazard area. For the most part building any structures within a 100 year flood plain is prohibited, and any requests to fill in the floodplain areas must be approved by FEMA and the local city, which can be a time-consuming process.

- **Impact fees**: Many cities impose park, road, school, utility, parking and other impact fees on new development, all of which can add substantial costs to a project. Early in the development process, and then throughout project planning, city staff should be asked, in writing, for a list of all impact fees and utility improvements that will be assessed against the project and these added costs should be factored into the project proforma.

- **Zoning letters/PZR reports**: To confirm that the site is properly zoned and entitled for the proposed use, either a zoning confirmation letter should be secured from the planning department of the city or a zoning report should be commissioned. All site development constraints should be determined, including setbacks from adjacent streets, building slope requirements, floor-area ratios (FAR) (the number of square feet of building allowed per square feet of land area), building heights, and open space requirements. The developer should confirm with the architect that all such building restrictions have been considered in designing the project. In some cities a development may "borrow" FAR from an adjacent site that is not fully utilizing its FAR through a density transfer that is recorded in the local real estate records.

- **Evidence of utilities**: Extensions and upsizing of utility lines can be expensive. To establish that utilities are available to and at the boundary of the site in sufficient capacity to serve the proposed project, an availability and capacity letter should be requested from the water, sewer, gas, cable TV/internet and electric providers. If utilities are not adjacent to the site or are not sized sufficiently for the proposed development, the developer should secure an estimate of the cost of extending or upsizing the utilities and include these costs in the development proforma.

- **Construction staging**: Particularly on tight urban sites, the developer will need to locate an adjacent tract of land to offload and store construction materials and place a construction office trailer. To the extent a lane on an adjacent street needs to be used to stage construction, the city will normally impose a fee for this temporary street closure and require an agreement with the developer on traffic and pedestrian safety protocol and repair of the street post-construction completion.

- **Replatting**: Some cities will require that the property be replatted before certain types of development can commence. Platting is a process by which the city reviews the proposed project and determines the impact on the city and on adjoining land uses, typically addressing issues like access along roads for the project and adjoining sites, traffic issues, fire lanes, etc. A preemptive meeting with the planning department will help to outline the schedule for city approvals.
- **Meetings with homeowners**: As stated previously, if the proposed project needs to be rezoned or has any potential for controversy, a meeting should be arranged with homeowners/property owners during the inspection period, and if it looks like a battle may ensue over the project, reconsider whether the time and energy would be better expended on another site.

It is not possible to overly emphasize the importance of doing detailed site due diligence, and the potential negative ramifications of failing to identify and resolve every open item or questionable finding. Zoning, environmental and survey/title issues can be particularly problematic, costly and time-consuming.

Amendments to the Purchase and Sale Agreement

During due diligence inspections and investigations, the developer may uncover obstacles that need to be overcome, such as:

- Restrictions affecting the proposed project.
- Project approvals or enhancements required from additional parties (e.g., homeowner or property owner associations).
- Political opposition to the proposed project.
- Environmental concerns that need to be cleaned up.
- Easements that traverse the land that need to be removed or rerouted.
- Utility or access easements that need to be secured from an adjoining parcel.
- Median breaks or curb cuts from adjoining roads.
- Existing tenants who refuse to be bought out.

Depending on the opposing parties' willingness to discuss solutions, the workaround may not be capable of agreement prior to the end of the inspection period. Resolving some obstacles to construction can be expensive (e.g., environmental cleanup) and may result in the buyer requesting that the seller bear these costs, and if the seller refuses termination of the contract may be the only solution. As these issues arise, early and consistent communication with the landowner is critical.

9 The Proforma
Running the Numbers

A thorough understanding of the financial proforma for a real development project requires a solid foundation in both Microsoft Excel and real estate finance—the hard science of spreadsheets and the soft science of the key financial metrics by which lenders and equity partners evaluate projects competing for financing. Most real estate developers start out as financial analysts—"Excel jocks" who understand how to set up the mathematical analysis of a real estate project and which variables can "move the needle" so that an infeasible project becomes feasible.

A word of warning—changing variables in a proforma is not magic. Merely manipulating the numbers that ultimately cannot be attained in development, construction or operation of the project can result in the developer not securing financing or incurring large financial losses.

Just dropping estimated project costs or increasing proposed rents or adding additional units can make a project seem feasible—however, all changes must be grounded in reality. If ultimately the project lender or equity partners scrub the numbers and determine that one or more factors in the proforma are not attainable, the developer will have wasted a lot of time, focus and money (pursuits costs and nonrefundable earnest money) chasing a rainbow. That said, comparisons cannot necessarily be made to projects that currently exist in the market if, for example, those projects are older, have poor design, lack amenities and services, etc. Adding analytics to the comparison may be helpful, preparing a chart that shows existing project characteristics—ages, amenities and services—and then quantifying the additional rent that could possibly be attained by the proposed project with better design and superior amenities and services than the older competitive properties. For instance, a developer in Dallas takes the position, justified by project performance over time, that their superior design and amenities for new projects attain 10% higher rents than the competition, and earn a lower cap rate (i.e., higher multiple of net earnings) on sale. Adding additional units can create an additional problem—once apartment projects push past 350 units, attaining full lease-up can be extremely hard, as units leased a year ago may now need to be released at the same time that trailing units are completed, resulting in "leasing into yourself," and until lease-up occurs permanent financing cannot be secured.

DOI: 10.1201/9781003264514-9

Although quantifying each variable is a helpful analytical step, in the end grasping the dynamics of a particular submarket is more art than science, and the analysis should always be tempered by a clear understanding of the fundamental nature of developers to be overly optimistic, pushing and pulling on the variables to make a project feasible.

As the proforma becomes more concrete, the development associate and financial analyst should present the project to senior company management in a "project review meeting," where everyone is encouraged to be constructively critical of project unit mixes, unit sizes, unit count, amenity and finish levels, proposed rents, anticipated construction and operational costs and project complexity/hurdles. Once the project is given the green light, predevelopment costs will mount quickly, with site pursuit and due diligence costs, hard earnest money and design professional fees easily topping a million dollars.

> *Periodic, planned, open debates around project viability could save the development company the heartache of writing off a large amount of dead deal costs later in the process, losses that could offset the gains on a successful project.*

Although a well-conceived real estate project Excel proforma can run into dozens of tabs, with a dizzying array of interrelated (and endlessly looping) computations, in the end there are only a few metrics that are critical to lenders and equity partners.

Key Metrics for Lenders

- **Loan-to-cost ratio** (LTC): The ratio of loan amount divided by the total development cost of the project. Most multifamily construction lenders will only finance 60–70% of project costs.
- **Loan-to-value ratio** (LTV): The ratio determined by dividing the construction loan amount by the as-built stabilized fair market value of the project, typically determined by an appraisal. Loans that have a high loan-to-value ratio are considered higher risk. As a benchmark, construction loans for apartment complex development tend to run 60–65% loan-to-value.
- **Debt service coverage ratio** (DSCR): The ratio of cash flow before debt service to the debt service payment, typically measured on an annual basis. On multifamily projects, lenders normally look for a DSCR of 1.1 to 1.0 or 1.2 to 1.0.
- **Debt yield**: The ratio of the project net operating income (typically as determined by the appraiser) divided the loan amount. Most multifamily lenders require a debt yield not less than 8.5:1.

Note, however, that lenders may be willing to fund construction loans with higher leverage if the developer has significant net worth and liquidity and is willing to guarantee a portion of the loan.

The Risk/Reward of Higher Leverage and Using "Other People's Money" (OPM)

Having more debt financing (and lower equity) is a double-edged sword, as additional leverage (more debt) increases the equity multiple and internal rate of return on invested capital but also increases the amount of risk to the developer, as lenders willing to loan a higher percentage of loan-to-cost (LTC) will require that some portion of the loan be guaranteed. Most loans at 60% LTC will not require a guaranty, but as LTC rises above 60% the construction lender may require that up to 50% of the loan be guaranteed, with the guaranty "burning off" in stages as the project becomes operational and reaches certain debt service coverage ratios (DSCRs).

The following table shows an over-simplified illustration of the potential upsides and risks of increasing leverage, using 60% leverage with no guaranty required, and 70% leverage, with the construction lender requiring the developer to guaranty 30% of the loan:

Capital stack:	60% leverage	70% leverage
Construction loan (1)	$ 60,000,000	$ 70,000,000
Equity (2)	$ 40,000,000	$ 30,000,000
Total project cost	$100,000,000	$100,000,000
Sales price	$ 120,000,000	$ 120,000,000
Less: project cost	($100,000,000)	($100,000,000)
Profit (3)	$ 20,000,000	$ 20,000,000
Return on equity (3)/(2)	50.00%	66.67%
Property value on foreclosure by lender (4)	$50,000,000	$50,000,000
Less: project cost	($100,000,000)	($100,000,000)
Loss on project	($50,000,000)	($50,000,000)
Lender loss (4)—(1)	$10,000,000	$20,000,000
Developer pays on guaranty	$0	$20,000,000

The risk/reward proposition of leverage is as follows: (a) if the project increases in value above project cost, higher leverage allows equity to earn a higher rate of return, but (b) if the project value falls below the loan amount, the developer/guarantor must pay the difference to the extent of the guaranteed portion of the loan. Although not illustrated above, if the project falls in value below the project cost, the developer and co-GP will bear the loss to a greater extent than the LP Partner, as the LP equity needs to returned off the top of any distributions on sale and the developer and co-GP will lose part or all of the Promote at the bottom of the distribution waterfall. Although lower leverage may return a lower return to the developer and its equity partners, a smaller loan amount that does not require a guaranty reduces the risk to the developer. Some LP equity partners may prod the developer to increase leverage to increase the internal rate of return to the LP partner, but developers should be wary of the increased guaranty risk typically associated with highly leveraged projects.

Key Metrics for Equity Partners

- **Equity multiple**: Institutional equity partners seek a multiple of their invested capital, simply determined by dividing the total amount of cash received by the amount invested. LP equity investors focus on this criteria as it is often not worth their time to evaluate and monitor an investment that does not, over time, return at last 2 times the amount invested. Co-GP partners take a higher level of risk by funding pre-development costs (and may actually incur dead deal costs on one project that needs to be offset by returns on later projects) and thus require a higher multiple return on their investment, often around a 4× to 5× multiple. Note, however, that equity multiple alone is not a very useful tool as it ignores the time value of money—a 2× multiple over 10 years does not have the same value as a 2× multiple over 5 years.
- **Rate of return** (ROR) on **total project cost**: Focuses on the ability of a project to generate sufficient cash flow on an annual basis to justify the investment, similar to an interest rate on a bond. ROR looks solely at operating cash flow and does not take into account any sales or refinancing proceeds. For potential multifamily projects, developers will not normally proceed unless the proforma stabilized cash flow generates a ROR in the range of 4.75–6.5%, with lower ROR rates in higher end East and West coast cities, mid-range ROR rates in other major metropolitan cities, and higher ROR rates in more third-tier markets.
- **Internal rate of return** (IRR) or **yield on invested capital** (sometimes referred to as the cash-on-cash return): IRR or yield takes into account the time value of money and in essence discounts back all cash flows (operational and sale or refinance) into present day, comparing those periodic cash flows to the amount invested (which also occurs over time), to determine the return rate on invested capital. The calculation is complex—but once learned the Microsoft Excel IRR function is the best, and most accepted, tool to determine IRR. LP equity investors typically look for cash-on-cash returns in the high-teens to low 20s.
- **Cost per unit** (sometimes referred to as "basis concerns"): With rising construction and land costs, equity investors also benchmark the project's cost per unit (for multifamily projects) or cost per square foot against recent sales of similar product. The equity partner's apprehension is that once the project is built, stabilized and put up for sale, purchasers will not be willing to pay more for the proposed project than the sales prices for existing projects, adjusting for some amount of inflation over the years from current day to the

date of proposed sale. This issue comes up most often when the developer is proposing a project that is "above the market" in terms of finish out and amenities, driving costs up, which may not ultimately result in a higher sales price on the back-end. If this occurs, the projected sales price may not be secured, and the investors' IRR will in reality be reduced.

10 Crafted Design, Urbanism and Green Buildings

In *The End of Secrets* (by Ryan Quinn) Kera, an FBI agent, is recruited out of the government to covertly spy on domestic targets. The ONE Corporation starts buying up media and entertainment companies, building up a stable of top performing artists in an attempt to massively commoditize their art/music by carefully engineering the "product"—the sound, the art, the media, the message. A number of their performers go missing, the supposed victims of suicide, murder or abduction and the intrigue begins. Kera and her hacker friends use computers and surveillance cameras around the city to spy on various persons of interest.

With rare exception, from the 1960s to the 1990s, real estate development in the United States was conceived, designed and built by developers operating like the ONE Corporation—treating real estate as a commodity, a financial instrument, something that could easily be understood on a nameless, faceless proforma. To meet the requirements of Wall Street and Big Banks, the product had to be contained within a certain box—high end neighborhoods, certain homogenous design, separation of uses, a certain number of units—so that they could slice and dice the debt and equity components of the investment into manageable chunks and sell it off to the masses—pension funds, life insurance companies, overseas investors, etc. We can't really blame the real estate development community—they were constrained by what was financeable and what the cities would let them build under (arcane) zoning and development codes that require separation of uses, to say nothing of "not in my backyard" pressures from homeowners if the new product was not the norm of surrounding uses. As long as federal, state and local governments built super-highways further out in the favored sectors, land was cheap and plentiful for this type of development.

Like in *The End of Secrets*, the process of commoditization murders the artists and destroys the art—in the case of cities, the art of placemaking. In contrast, great places, like great art, inspire us and make an impression for decades and have lasting value.

> **We can simply walk away from bad art—a bad real estate project has a 100-year impact on the surrounding area that is hard to remedy.**

DOI: 10.1201/9781003264514-10

Figure 10.1 Walkable Street

Source: photo courtesy of Ian Freimuth, Creative Commons

There are also economic reasons why developers should endeavor to create bet-ter projects. A well-designed and located project will garner higher rents and be more profitable to the developer, GP Partner and LP Partner. Areas that have high Walk Scores[1]—that are walkable and bikeable, with easy access to grocer-ies, restaurants, errands, parks and cultural attractions—are more desirable to tenants, are typically more sought after by large capital partners, and ultimately secure lower cap rates / higher sales prices for the developer.

Residents will pay for what they can "touch and feel." Ambiance, textures, smells, quality of materials, art and other high design elements such as quality furniture in common areas, crown moldings, and trayed ceilings with backlight-ing are equally as valuable to renters as homeowners, creating a sense of home versus just a temporary apartment box. Every project should make a statement in its exterior, common spaces and user spaces. Innovate, don't replicate. Higher value (and profit to the developer) comes from unique design, enhancing how the end user experiences the project, the immersive emotion that the place invokes. Function is important to use, but design is critical to experience—and people pay for experience. A "great building" is a creative and collaborative combination of urban planning, architecture, interior design and landscape architecture. This creativity can be applied to a suburban garden style apartment complex as well as an upscale urban high rise, although the design aesthetics and cost (and the ultimate impact of cost on the rent to be paid by the consumer) must be tuned to what is acceptable and affordable to the local audience.

The project should not just be designed—it should be crafted to create a beautiful place that is truly valued by the community. To enhance the aesthetics of the project, the exterior of the building should be compatible with and integrate into the surrounding neighborhood. Taller buildings should have top, middle and bottom architectural features to draw the eyes from vertical to horizontal, as monolithic buildings smother the surrounding area. The first two or three floors of any tall building are the focal points for the average pedestrian, cyclist or car traveler, and extra care should be taken in designing those areas, including larger floor plates and doorways or *porte cocheres* along the ground floor, with a landscaped, tree-lined buffer between the street and the sidewalk, all purposefully designed to create a sense of arrival and human scale along the main building facade. Where possible after the first two floors the building should tier back away from the street to avoid a tall canyon effect along the street. Inset balconies are preferable to "bolt on" balconies on large footprint big box projects. External materials and colors should be arranged to create compatible variation and break up large facades with building articulation.

> A building by itself is not architecture—it is form or sculpture. Architecture is the interplay between life and form. The forms influence our way of using cities. Though it is easy to study form, it is really much more complicated to study life and the interaction between form and life.
>
> Jan Gehl[2]

Stated another way, an apartment building is not just a pretty object, nor is it a collection of residential units—it is a place where people live and experience their lives, and every project should enhance life, should enhance that experience, both for the residents and the surrounding community.

Parking garages and other block walls should be positioned away from the main street, and should be screened or contain architectural features to break up the scale. To the extent that the surrounding area is walkable to retail, restaurants or mass transit, the developer should consider reducing the number of parking spaces if allowed by local building codes, working toward a less car-dependent lifestyle for the residents. Above-ground parking cost between $12,000 and $15,000 per parking space, and below-grade parking averages between $25,000 and $35,000 per space, making reductions in parking a prime target for bringing a project into budget.

Storage has become a key component of any apartment project. Apartment residents, and particularly "renters by choice" who have sold their large homes and decide to rent rather than own, need a significant amount of storage space. Added kitchen, laundry room, bathroom and water closet storage are necessities. Using otherwise dead space in a building (for instance, behind elevator shafts or stair towers) or creating a few parking garages with added storage space is a simple means to create ancillary project income, as tenants will pay a premium for easily accessible storage space within the building versus driving to a third party storage facility. Adequate secure bicycle parking should be well-placed and considered in the early parking design, and with the increasing popularity of plug-in hybrid and electric cars, charging stations should be in place when the project opens, and sleeving inserted for future charging station infrastructure.

Common areas within the building should be designed with the purpose of creating community in mind and with the expectation that these community spaces become an extension of the residents' units. Renters who form new friend-ships within the property tend to be less likely to move, reducing turn-over and the cost of vacancies, make-ready expenses and leasing commissions. Coffee bars should not just be afterthoughts in the lobby, but should be located near com-fortable gathering places. With apartment dwellers living in smaller spaces than homeowners, residents need common areas that can be reserved for gatherings of family and friends, and even areas to work outside their units.

All of these design elements increase development costs, and ultimately the project proforma must be balanced between added cost, additional rent poten-tial and meeting financing metrics so that the project is financeable. Will the residents pay more for the added amenities and design improvements? Will the resulting rents push the market too far, such that lenders and equity partners lose faith in the above-market rent needed to support the added cost? That said, imaginative design elements can be included in any budget, and even in less expensive rental markets residents will pay extra for certain amenities.

If more developers would take the time to consider the importance of design and contextual fit within the surrounding community, we could begin to chip away at the "not in my backyard" prejudice against apartments by adding to rather than subtracting from the vibrancy and livability of the community. Developers need to think outside the box of their project, and entertain the notion that their civic responsibility is to raise the quality of life and standard of living in the neighborhood by crafting better places to live, work and play.

Equity partners in the last 10 years have become increasingly focused on invest-ing in environmentally sustainable buildings designed to reduce energy and water use or use more passive forms of energy. Attaining an actual environmental certi-fication such as a Leadership in Energy and Environmental Design (LEED) rating is an expensive, time-consuming and cumbersome process, and some argue is a too formalistic "check the box" routine that doesn't really add value to a project, but the scope of all architectural engagements should incorporate ecologically sensitive materials and design elements into a project in a cost-effective manner. Early in the project financing process the developer should ask prospective equity partners to provide their green building standards. Oftentimes equity partners are willing to alter their economic terms with developers in exchange for incurring added costs to comply with green building requirements.

Notes

1 www.walkscore.com
2 Jan Gehl, "In Search of the Human Scale," www.youtube.com/watch?v=Cgw9oHDfJ4k

11 Value Engineering and the Design/Build Process

As the project moves from concept and due diligence to architectural and engineering planning, an initial discussion with the potential contractor can prove highly beneficial. One of the most frustrating aspects of development and construction occurs when construction bids are above the budget and the project, which has been in the works for months, suddenly seems unfeasible as rents will not support the higher construction cost. The fallback remedy is always "value engineering," a pejorative term for reducing amenities, picking lower-cost materials, and possibly redrawing the project. A brick building suddenly has more stucco; granite countertops give way to Formica; wood flooring becomes vinyl laminate; cheaper light fixtures, cabinetry and faucets are chosen, all of which create a risk of potential clashes with the city and homeowners when the shared high-end vision becomes stark budget reality. Changes to design quality ultimately also lead to reductions in revenue, as a B quality project won't garner the same rents as an A quality project, which spirals back to a re-analysis of project feasibility. At this point, design plans may also have been shared with potential equity partners, who have locked into the project vision and will be reluctant to reduce project quality. Value engineering literally happens when the project is otherwise almost ready to start, and will delay the project by months, demoralizing all who have worked on the project.

Value engineering chaos can be largely overcome up-front in the development cycle by embracing a design/build process, where the probable contractor and key subcontractors are actively involved with the team during each phase of plan development, particularly early in the planning process to both suggest alternatives to keep the project on budget and also to identify errors in the plans (which may otherwise only be found during actual construction) or "over-engineering" of the plans where less expensive alternative construction methods could be employed. The downside of design/build is that, if the developer does not have its own internal contractor, the most suitable third-party contractor (the "design/build contractor") must be chosen up-front, leading that contractor to act as if they have already been selected as the project contractor and potentially lowering the incentives for the contractor to be budget conscious

DOI: 10.1201/9781003264514-11

in pricing. To mitigate this risk, engage a trusted contractor that has built projects previously for your company (or who comes highly recommended by other developers) early in the design process and inform that contractor that it has not been selected to build the project, but has a leg up on the competition when the project is bid out by being involved in the design/build process.

12 Owner–Architect Agreement

The owner–architect agreement (the "OA agreement") establishes the parameters by which the architect designs the project and the responsibilities of the architect to the owner. In very broad terms, this agreement obligates the architect to design the project in compliance with applicable zoning laws and building codes through certain "design phases," with corresponding payments from the owner based on percentage of completion of each phase. Although there is an American Institute of Architects (AIA) form of OA agreement, sophisticated developers will opt to use a form scripted from scratch, as unsurprisingly the AIA form grants an unusual amount of project decision making authority to the architect. Most development attorneys have created their own more balanced forms of OA agreement, and I would strongly recommend using a scripted form drafted by developer's counsel and negotiated with the architect. Most developers engage a limited number of architects, and once the form of OA agreement is agreed to that document can be used as the template for future projects.

A well-drafted OA agreement will address the following issues:

- **Compensation**: The payments from owner to architect during the various phases of plan development, reimbursable and non-reimbursable expenses and hourly rates for additional services.
- **Consultants**: In general all of the other design consultants, other than possibly landscaping and interior design, should be housed "under" the architect (sometimes referred to as "subconsultants")—i.e., the architect hires the consultants and manages and coordinates their work with the architect's plans. To the extent the owner directly engages owner consultants, the architect should be required to incorporate and coordinate all drawings provided by the owner consultants with the architect's drawings. Subconsultant agreements should require certain minimum amounts of professional liability insurance and should name the owner as a third party beneficiary of such agreements.
- **Representatives**: To avoid too many decision makers pulling the architect in multiple directions, the owner should name one person who is in charge of

DOI: 10.1201/9781003264514-12

all discussions with the architect. The owner and architect should agree on which architect design professional should serve as the principal architect, and another architect as project manager. The architect should be allowed to substitute another principal architect or project manager only with the owner's approval.

- **Timing of plan production**: A schedule of plan development should be an exhibit to the OA Agreement, and the architect should comply with the schedule. In most cases the owner will not close on the acquisition of the project site until the plans have been fully completed, project construction pricing has been secured and financing has been obtained—and the owner is operating under a purchase contract deadline to close the site. Timely completion of the plans is critical to this sequence of events.
- **Meetings**: The architect's scope of services should include attendance at project meetings or conference calls and presentations of the project to the city and neighborhood groups.
- **Subordinations and certificates**: The project architect and all subconsultants and owner consultants should be required to deliver to the owner, lender and equity partners any subordinations or certificates reasonably required by such parties.
- **Water proofing**: The architect should be required to hire a waterproofing consultant, to incorporate the consultant's recommendations into the project plans, and be responsible for water proofing inspections and details.
- **Revisions to plans to meet budget**: At the end of the schematic design phase, the owner either internally with its own construction estimators, or with the assistance of one of the prospective contractors, arrives at a proposed construction cost budget for the project. The architect should then design to that budget in future iterations of the plans. The architect's scope of services and compensation should include any redesign of the project to stay within the budget, without additional charge.
- **Construction administration**: As the contractor begins construction of the project, various building trades will submit shop drawings that drill into the details of various construction elements. Examples include floor joints and roof trusses, heating, ventilation and air conditioning (HVAC) systems, and fire/life safety systems. The OA agreement should provide that the architect will review these drawings for consistency with the overall design intent and will sign off on the shop drawings. In addition, as the project is being constructed the architect should attend project meetings with the owner and contractor not less frequently than monthly, and should, as part of the monthly construction draw process, certify to the owner, project lenders and equity partners the percentage of completion of each construction trade. If the architect notices any deviation of project construction from the plans, the architect should notify the owner. Upon substantial completion of the project, the architect and owner normally create a punch-list of unfinished items for the attention of the contractor,

and the architect issues a certificate of substantial completion using AIA Document G704, to satisfy lender and equity partner requirements that substantial completion has been attained by the required completion deadlines in the construction loan agreement and the limited partner equity joint venture agreement.

13 Development Planning Phases

Once the preliminary proforma shows the project meets or is close to meeting required financial metrics, the project can move forward with the next, lengthy and costly phases—crafting the architectural and engineering plans—which can easily cost over $1 million and take 9–12 months to complete.

Architects typically break down the planning phase into five subparts:

- **Schematic design** (SD phase): Schematic design lays out the basics of the core and exterior or the project, without really delving into interior design. The exterior form of the building(s) is established; the interior units or square feet are roughly approximated; exterior access points are located and materials are described. To facilitate any political efforts like rezoning or meetings with homeowners' or property owners' associations, a colored rendering of the project may be prepared by the architect or a graphic designer. As schematic design proceeds, the developer should meet with the city planning department to ascertain that all local zoning and other site constraints are accounted for in the site plan for the project.
- **Design drawings** (DD phase): The design drawings are more detailed, laying out the entire interior of the project, including details like mechanical, electrical and plumbing (MEP) layouts; cabinet locations; office and amenities; elevator cores and stairwells; etc. The details of particular material specifications are not normally determined at this point, but with a general grade of materials quality preliminary construction pricing ("DD pricing") can be secured upon DD's reaching 70–80% completion.
- **Construction drawings** (CD phase): Construction drawings contain all the details necessary to actually build the project, including a full set of specifications—listing specific material, supply and equipment providers and manufacturers. The "spec book" can run into hundreds of pages with precise materials listings: product numbers and manufacturers for light switches, washer/dryers and plumbing fixtures; doors; trims; windows; ceiling fans; air conditioning units; etc. After the CD's are prepared, the contractor should update the construction cost bid and provide a formal guaranteed maximum price (GMP) construction contract—actual construction costs

DOI: 10.1201/9781003264514-13

plus a fee (that includes the contractor's overhead) with a cost not to exceed a stated maximum price.

- **Permit set**: After the CDs are prepared and refined through discussions with the developer, the architect will prepare the "permit set" of plans that are submitted to the city for comments prior to a building permit being issued. Cities normally require multiple copies of the permit plans, and comments are provided by various city departments, including planning, engineering, traffic planning and fire department. At this stage, the city should also provide a more comprehensive statement of impact fees that may be assessed against the project.
- **Issued for construction plans** (the "IFC set"): After the architect and developer have responded to all of the city comments, the architect will issue the IFC plans, a final set of plans that are the playbook by which the general contractor builds the project.

At each stage of plan development, the developer, the design/build contractor and key subcontractors should carefully review the plans to ascertain that all desired design elements have been included, and update and review the budget and suggest alternatives means and materials to keep the project on budget.

14 Project Financing

Financing Overview

Understanding real estate development finance starts at a very high level and is best illustrated with an example. Let's assume we are developing a $100 million multifamily project. Typical financing involves a layering of various financial sources referred to as the "capital stack" as follows:

Construction Loan (60% loan to cost)	$60,000,000
Limited Partner Equity (90% of equity)	$36,000,000
General Partner Equity:	
- Co-GP Partner (90% of balance)	$ 3,600,000
- Developer Equity (remainder)	$ 400,000

Note that the percentages above are estimates:

- The construction loan amount could be higher, particularly if the developer is willing to guaranty a portion of the loan.
- Limited partner equity could be lower, particularly if the developer wants a higher Promote.
- The Co-GP equity could be lower, depending on the waterfall of profits between the developer and the co-GP partner.

Financing Package

Once the design development plans are approximately 70–80% complete and the contractor submits preliminary pricing, the proforma is updated, and if the project meets debt and equity required financing metrics, the developer can begin the process of securing equity financing. Developer staff will prepare a pitch book, referred to as the financing package, typically containing the following materials:

- Cover page with the developer logo and a rendering of the project.
- Project summary.

DOI: 10.1201/9781003264514-14

- Market research on the area (job growth, surrounding development, access to amenities, area rent comparables).
- Summary of project proforma financial performance and returns to the investors, indicating how the project meets financial metrics.
- Pictures of prior projects developed and a summary of financing results (returns to the investors) of those projects, highlighting the developer's track record.
- Developer resume and bios of key personnel.

If the development company has an in-house finance team and prior debt and equity relationships, financing may be secured using in-house resources. Alternatively, outside financing brokers such as CBRE, JLL, Northmarq or Eastdil may be engaged to broadcast the pitchbook to a wider audience of financing sources. Broker financing commissions typically average around 1% of the funding secured by the broker, and it is common to either exclude from the brokerage agreement certain financing sources that the developer has engaged in the past, or to pay the broker a reduced commission if the financing is secured from one of the excluded sources.

Co-General Partner Equity

As indicated in the table above, without a co-general partner, the developer's capital contribution to a $100 million project would be $4,000,000, and if the developer is invested in or pursuing multiple projects the amount of invested or committed developer capital can become massive. Additionally, before construction of a project commences, if the developer does not have a co-GP, the developer bears the entire burden of pursuit costs (e.g., earnest money deposits, legal fees, professional property investigation expenses and design fees), which can run well over $1 million per project. Although these amounts are substantially "trued up" with (reimbursed by) the limited partner equity at closing, a developer who is simultaneously pursuing multiple projects will have large amounts of pursuit cost exposure over a significant time frame.

Most development companies prefer to use "other people's money" (OPM) to the maximum extent possible, in order to (i) reduce the required contributions from developer principals and (ii) create more leverage, being the opportunity to earn greater profits with less capital, increasing the IRR and return multiple on developer principal capital as the developer retains an outsized portion of the Promote as versus the amount shared with the co-GP partner. Without co-GP funds, the return on developer capital may only average a 3× or 5× multiple, whereas with co-GP funds, the right sharing ratio and a well performing project the multiple could be 7× to 20×.

For these reasons, many development companies have a co-GP partner that provides the majority of the pursuit costs, predevelopment funding and general partner equity required for the various projects that are being investigated, pursued and developed. Co-GP partners are typically investing either foreign funds or the holdings of very high net worth individuals or family offices and require high rates of return (20–30% annual IRR and 5× to 10× multiples) for taking greater real estate risks.

A typical co-GP structure is exhibited in Figure 14.1. As briefly outlined above, the developer normally shares some of the Promote with the co-GP partner, but the developer's share is disproportionately large as compared to the amount of capital provided by the developer versus the co-GP partner. The amount of Promote that the co-GP can demand depends on the track record of the developer, the level of participation the developer requires in predevelopment costs and whether the developer also asks the co-GP partner to help fund general operational costs of the development company (such as salaries and other overhead)—and typically varies from sharing 20% to 50% of the promote. The profits distribution provisions between the developer and co-GP partner might look something like the following, assuming the co-GP partner is contributing 80% of the GP capital:

• **Distributions other than with respect to Promote**: Cash flow other than with respect to Promote received from the project owner by the joint venture between the developer and the co-GP (this "JV") will be distributed *pari passu* to the members based on their capital contribution percentages (i.e., 20% to the developer and 80% to the co-GP).
• **Distributions of Promote**: Cash flow arising from the Promote received from the project owner by this JV will be distributed to the members 75% to the developer and 25% to the co-GP.

Co-GP partners provide "high risk" capital, sometimes referred to as being at the top of the capital stack. If there is a default by the developer in its obligations to the institutional capital partner, either as the managing member of the project owner, as developer or as contractor (if an affiliate of the developer also serves as

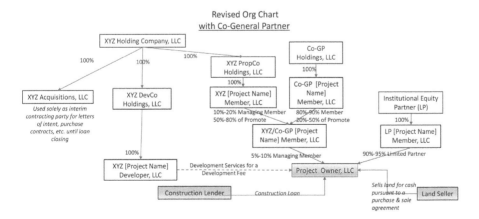

Figure 14.1 Revised Organizational Chart 14.1 – with Co-General Partner

the general contractor for the project), the developer is typically penalized and will lose its Promote distribution—which in turns results in the co-GP losing its interest in the Promote (which the co-GP may then require to be reimbursed by the principals of the developer if the loss of Promote is due to developer bad acts). Although the developer serves as the managing member of the JV between the developer and co-GP partner, given the potential for the co-GP to lose its share of the Promote standard co-GP joint venture provisions have a laundry list of "major decisions"—areas where the developer as managing member may only take action with approval of the co-GP partner. Term sheets and joint venture agreements with Co-GP partners are extremely complicated, and legal counsel with extensive experience in equity joint venture agreements should be employed early in the negotiation process.

Developers with a strong track record and strong relationships with high-net-worth individuals (or their family offices) may take a different approach that could result in the developer keeping all or a larger share of the Promote, thus dramatically increasing the developer's multiple on its invested funds. Instead of bringing in a co-GP partner, the developer syndicates, through a private placement memorandum, a share of the developer's interest in the "Distributions other than with respect to Promote." This financing is possible as most high net worth individuals do not have access to invest in co-GP funds, and can't even earn the rates of return, particularly in today's low interest rate environment, that even limited partner investors earn in real estate development transactions. Most high net worth individuals will settle for an 18–20% IRR on their funds, which in most financeable real estate developments can be earned just from the "distributions other than with respect to Promote." If that hurdle can't be met, the developer could also agree to share a small portion of the Promote with the syndicate of high net worth individuals. The downside to the developer is that these syndicated investors do not also contribute toward predevelopment costs or developer operating funding, such that these investor pools normally work best for projects where there is very little predevelopment funding needed or such amounts have already been spent and closing is imminent.

Syndicated GP Equity

Securities laws generally require that equity only be syndicated to "accredited investors"—mainly high net worth or high-income individuals/couples who meet one of the following two criteria:

- Income: for an individual $200,000 (and for a couple, $300,000) or more for two of the past three years and likely to make the same amount this year; *or*
- Assets: net worth of over $1 million excluding primary residence.

An offering document called a private placement memorandum ("PPM") should be prepared by a corporate attorney with a solid understanding of federal and state securities laws. PPMs serve two purposes that are held in dynamic tension: informing the potential investor of the risks of investing in the project, while marketing the investment opportunity. The offering document summarizes the project; discusses the background of the developer as managing member or general partner of the investment entity along with the authority of the developer to act on behalf of the venture; outlines the organizational structure of the project entities; sets out the track record of the developer and its principals; establishes the potential investment returns to the investors; and, most importantly, describes in detail the potential risks to the investors, including that the investment return may not be earned and the scenarios under which the investors could lose their entire investment. The organizational document (limited liability company agreement or limited partnership agreement) and an investor questionnaire, where the investor certifies his or her status as an accredited investor, are attached to the PPM.

Co-GP Partner with Syndicated Developer Piece

Finally, as to GP funding there is another wrinkle, where both a co-GP partner and a syndicated investment pool are part of the structure. This dual GP level funding can arise in several scenarios: (i) where the limited partner and the co-GP partner both reduce the amount of capital that they are willing to contribute to the project, and the developer uses a syndicated pool of sophisticated investors to fill the equity gap, or (ii) where the project has a higher total capitalization, and the amount of the developer required capital exceeds the amount that the developer is willing to contribute.

LP and Co-GP Capital Commitment ($100 million project)

Construction Loan (60% loan to cost)	$60,000,000
Limited Partner Equity (80% of equity)	$32,000,000
General Partner Equity:	
- Co-GP Partner (80% of balance)	$ 6,400,000
- Developer Equity (remainder)	$ 1,600,000

The reduction in LP equity and GP equity, as compared to the example on page 51, results in the Developer Equity increasing by $1,200,000 (from $400,000 to $1,600,000). Most developers are not willing to contribute such a large amount of equity to any one project, and one solution is to syndicate out the extra $1,200,000 of equity.

Total Project Cost Increases to $150 million

Construction Loan (60% loan to cost)	$90,000,000
Limited Partner Equity (90% of equity)	$54,000,000
General Partner Equity:	
- Co-GP Partner (90% of balance)	$ 5,400,000
- Developer Equity (remainder)	$ 600,000

The 50% increase in project cost elevates the developer's required contribution by 50% (from $400,000 to $600,000), which may result in the developer determining to cap its contributions at a lower amount, and syndicate out the additional equity required.

The organizational chart becomes even more complex with both a co-GP partner and syndicating part of the developer equity (Figure 14.2). Obviously, adding additional parties to the transaction adds additional legal documentation, not only with the added parties, but also between the various financing sources. For instance, in most cases co-GP partners have the right to remove and replace the developer, as managing member of the joint venture between the developer and the co-GP partner, if the developer commits certain bad acts such as fraud or intentional negligence or if a key developer principal is convicted of a felony. These removal rights will be problematic for the limited partner capital provider, who is providing the vast majority of the equity for the project, and will not be acceptable to the construction lender that is relying on the experience of the developer, resulting in extensive negotiations over these removal and step-in rights. As layers of financing are added, and particularly if the project involves a mixture of uses with multiple developers, complexity and chaos creep in—the number of law firms involved increases, the documentation checklist expands,

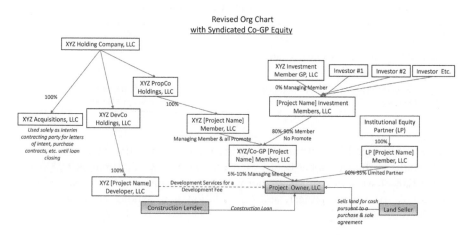

Figure 14.2 Revised Organizational Chart 14.2 – with Syndicated Co-GP Equity

more parties are examining the added relationships and suddenly weekly conference calls are calendered with 5 sets of attorneys and their clients.

> *Early in the project progression, as the developer begins to see this drama unfold, a quick reevaluation should be made as to whether the costs, risks and—most importantly—the time and energy investment is worth the potential reward. Is the thrill of the complexity and the project "cool factor" driving the decision, or economically is this really worth the effort?*

Limited Partner Equity

The vast majority of equity for real estate projects comes from life insurance companies (e.g., Prudential or MetLife) and major non-bank financial companies (e.g., Carlyle and Goldman Sachs). The joint venture agreements for limited partner (LP) equity vary—in most cases the developer serves as the managing member or general partner of the venture, but occasionally the equity partner is the managing member, with the developer being an "administrative member," with significant rights during construction of the project but limited rights thereafter. In either case, the limited partner equity provider will have approval rights over all major decisions—identity of and terms with lenders; significant borrowing; terms of and execution of major contracts; material alterations of the project or the project budget; etc. Basically, all decisions that could have a material impact on the project or the limited partner's rights are subject to their approval.

LP partners are mostly represented by large law firms out of Boston, New York or Chicago and negotiations with a new LP partner can take months, involving joint venture agreements that run over 100 pages, with separate development agreements, construction contracts and ancillary documents. LP equity will also review and comment on the agreement with the GP partner, title and survey and all property and project due diligence, typically will require architectural changes and may require reductions or additions to the project budget. The developer should hire counsel that is highly experienced with negotiating with institutional equity partners. Among the more significant provisions to discuss with LP equity are:

- **Major decisions**: What leeway does the developer have to make architectural, development, construction and operational changes without LP approval?
- **Sharing in pre-development costs**: As mentioned previously, developers normally have a finite amount of funds to invest in projects and therefore need to use financial leverage from both co-GP and LP partners. Many LP investors will not assist with funding predevelopment costs, preferring to put in their capital once the project is ready to start construction, as funding their capital later increases the IRR on their investment due to their money being invested for a shorter time period between investment and return on investment. However, once a relationship has been created with an

institutional investor they may be open to creating a programmatic relationship to facilitate consistent deal flow from the developer, including assisting in funding predevelopment costs but at a reduced rate (e.g., 50% of predevelopment costs vs. truing up to and funding at 90% of equity after construction commencement).

- **Capital contribution percentages**: For purposes of the discussion below, assume that the LP partner is contributing 90% of the capital and the developer is contributing 10%.
- **Distribution waterfall**: Profits are normally shared between the developer (and its co-GP partner) and the LP partner based on a tiered "waterfall." For instance, distributions could be made as follows—(i) to the LP partner and the developer *pari passu* (i.e., based on their capital contributions or 90%/10%) until the partners each receive a 9% internal rate of return (IRR) on and of their capital; (ii) 80% to the LP partner/20% to the developer until the LP partner has received a 12% IRR on its investment; (iii) 70% to the LP partner and 30% to the developer until the LP partner has received a 15% IRR on its investment; (iv) 60% to the LP partner and 40% to the developer until the LP partner has received an 18% IRR on its investment; and (v) 50% to the LP partner and 50% to the developer thereafter. The LP partner will push for higher IRR hurdles and for the developer to receive a lower percentage at the "bottom" of the waterfall, while the developer will vie for a greater share of the profits and a higher sharing ratio at the bottom of the waterfall. Note that in this example the developer's Promote, using the 90%/10% assumed capital contributions, would be all distributions that the developer receives that are in excess of 10% of the total distributions.
- **Consequences of developer bad acts**: Institutional equity partners engage with a fairly limited number of developers who they trust have the experience and personnel to develop, construct and manage the project, and they frequently have a programmatic relationship with those developers, where the developers show each of their projects to a small set of equity investors resulting in multiple projects with each of their stable of equity investors. As a result, the interaction between the LP partner and the developer is personal. Any breach of trust by the developer and any change in key personnel becomes problematic for the investor. LP partners will demand very punitive measures for any bad acts by the developer, such as the ability to remove the developer as the managing member of the partnership and in cases involving fraud, gross negligence or intentional misconduct will likely require the developer to forfeit its Promote. Additionally, the joint venture agreement with the LP partner may also propose a loss of Promote if key developer personnel are charged with or convicted of a felony. Developer's counsel should carefully review these provisions, and limit the investor's enforcement rights to bad acts that have a material adverse effect on the project, allow the developer to cure bad acts by non-executive personnel by reimbursing the joint venture and firing the problematic employee, and

restrict felony remedies to only critical executives convicted of (and not just charged with) felonies involving moral turpitude.

- **Timing of payment of developer fees**: The LP investor's initial proposal may be to pay the developer fee 90% over the course of construction, with the remaining 10% paid upon issuance of final certificates of occupancy (COs). When construction starts, the developer will likely have spent one year or longer pursuing the project, expending vast amounts of time, energy and money. LP investors normally will allow 20–25% of the developer fee to be paid on construction commencement, with 65–70% then paid *pari passu* with construction draws, and the final 10% paid when the final certificates of occupancy are received.

- **Funding of cost overruns**: Most LP partners take the position that any development costs in excess of the development budget (i.e., cost overruns) are the sole responsibility of the developer, do not constitute capital contributions and will not either earn a rate of return or be returned in the distribution waterfall. Some investors will contribute toward "uncontrollable" cost overruns—those that could not have been foreseen or controlled by the developer, such as environmental conditions that were not revealed by environmental reports or hidden underground rock that was not identified in the soils report—however, even if the investor does contribute to uncontrollable costs, they are likely to contribute a smaller share of these costs (e.g., 50%–50% with the developer instead of 90%–10%) and these contributions may be returnable in the waterfall after only normal equity is paid back with its return rates. Cost overruns are the Achilles' heel for developers—when they occur, the amount can be large and can easily eliminate the developer's Promote and/or equity contributions. With the co-GP partner being aligned with the developer, their counsel will also be keenly interested in cost overrun provisions. Experienced developer counsel can help negotiate the most-favorable treatment of cost overruns.

- **Loan guarantees, capital calls and indemnification of the developer**: The developer will be required to sign several loan guarantees—a guaranty of completion of the project and a nonrecourse carveout (bad boy) guaranty at a minimum, and if the loan has a higher than normal loan-to-cost ratio, a guaranty of a certain amount of the principal of the loan (e.g., 25% or 50%). In what circumstances should the LP partner participate in (sometimes referred to as "indemnify the developer for") any payments the developer is required to make to the lender under these guarantees? At a minimum, the developer should require the LP partner to pay its share of any non-controllable project costs that cause liability to the developer under the guarantees, such as subsurface soil conditions or environmental problems. Recently lumber and steel prices have spiked, and many contractors are excluding increases in these materials from their guaranteed maximum price contracts. Rising materials costs are another area where the LP partner should be encouraged to participate, although most investors will resist this request and demand that the developer or contractor bear this risk.

- **Completion guarantees to LP partner and liquidated damages**: If an affiliate of the developer serves as the general contractor, the LP partner may require a credit-worthy affiliate of the developer to guaranty the obligations of the contractor, and will require the contractor to pay liquidated damages for late delivery of the project. The developer should not, however, agree to backstop events that cannot be controlled, such as hidden soil conditions, environmental conditions, supply disruptions and other events of force majeure. One word of caution on completion deadlines—contractors (whether independent or affiliates of the developer) frequently miss completion deadlines, and a sufficient "buffer" should be built into the completion schedule to protect the developer against becoming obligated for substantial liquidated damages.

- **Budget reallocations and use of contingency**: When the development budget is created many construction line items have not been fully "bought out" (contracted for) by the contractor, a large percentage of soft costs will not yet have been incurred or committed, and the developer needs the ability to reallocate any unused line item to other areas where a budgeted line item may be exceeded. The LP partner may push to restrict reallocation, but the developer should respond that (i) the developer's authority to reallocate will be restricted by the construction loan agreement, and (ii) the economic deal with the LP partner is delivery of the project for a fixed amount of investment by the LP partner, and the LP partner is not therefore harmed by the developer reallocating the budget to cover legitimate cost overruns.

- **Crystallization and forced sale rights**: The capital provided by the LP partner has a "meter" (rate of return) that keeps running until the LP partner's capital is repaid, and the developer's Promote does not get paid until after the LP partner's capital and accrued return are paid out. Sale of the project will be a major decision requiring LP partner approval, putting the LP partner in control of the timing of the repayment of its capital, such that the developer's Promote can end being "buried behind" the LP meter. The LP partner may also have a different thought process on its investment horizon, preferring a long-term hold whereas the developer may want to build/stabilize/sell. One creative solution to this inherent tension is for the developer to have the right, within a certain period of time (say 1–2 years) after project stabilization, to "crystallize" the Promote—that is, to force a valuation of the project, run that valuation through the waterfall to determine the relative percentage of the proceeds that would be paid to the developer versus the LP partner (in essence determining "ownership" of the project), and then amend the joint venture agreement to eliminate the waterfall and just set ownership in the determined percentages. Only around one-half of the institutional investors will allow crystallization, but the developer should prefer this strategy as it allows the developer the ability to stay invested in the project if a long-term hold is desired—there are some locations and assets that are irreplaceable, and the savvy developer will engineer a solution that holds onto these projects. If the LP partner is unwilling to allow crystallization, an alternative strategy would be for the developer to have the right to force a sale of the project post-stabilization. The LP partner would then have the ability to either buy-out the developer based on a valuation, or it can instead put the project up for sale.

- **Competing projects and right of first offer**: Understandably, LP partners do not want their development partners to build competing projects, and also want to be involved in future phases of development within any larger master-planned area where the current project is being developed. The natural tendency of LP partners and their legal counsel is to draft heavy handed, far reaching non-competition clauses that include expansive non-compete areas (i.e., the entire city or a 5 mile radius) for the entire period during which the LP partner holds an interest in the project. The developer needs to protect its ability to continue to create projects in the prime areas of major metropolitan areas while still being respectful of the LP partner's valid concerns. A properly limited non-compete would (i) allow the LP partner to participate in future phases on a right of first offer basis as described below, and (ii) allow the developer to proceed with other projects in the non-compete area once the current project starts leasing activities (as the subsequent project construction will take at least 18 months or so, allowing the current project sufficient head start). The right of first offer allows the LP partner to have the first right to propose the terms of investment in competing projects, and if the developer rejects those terms, the developer can only then accept another investor's proposal on terms that are materially more favorable to the developer.

Equity Types and Return Expectations

In general, equity that takes more risk (e.g., co-GP equity that shares in pursuit risk) requires a greater reward, with the flip side being that equity that comes in at construction loan closing (LP equity or syndicated GP equity) will accept a lower rate of return. To conceptualize the various risk profiles: (i) if the construction lender takes back the project, all the equity is lost—so equity is higher risk and the construction loan is lower risk as it has the first right to the value of the project. If the LP Partner takes back the project, the construction loan stays in place, but the GP and developer equity is lost, making the GP and developer equity a higher risk investment than the LP equity. The developer is at risk of losing his equity (and time, emotional energy and opportunity cost) to anyone taking less risk—which is why the developer has the highest rate of return.

Construction Loan Financing

Sourcing a construction loan normally occurs after LP equity financing is secured and the contractor has provided preliminary construction pricing, allowing refinement of the development budget. When an equity partner is already in place, construction lenders feel more comfortable that a project will proceed.

Once a construction lender sizes its loan, increases to the loan amount will likely require additional loan committee approval, and loan officers are typically reluctant to go back to committee.

For larger construction loans, lenders will typically either participate out the loan or the lead lender will "syndicate" the loan. In a participation, the lead lender makes the loan and the participants merely fund a portion of the loan and have an interest in the overall loan—the other lenders do not have a direct relationship with the borrower. In a syndication, the lead lender only funds a portion of the loan (typically more than 50%) and other lenders fund side-by-side loans for the balance. Each lender has a separate promissory note from the borrower, but the lenders share one deed of trust or mortgage lien against the project—with the lead lender managing the security interest for the benefit of all lenders. A syndication is riskier for the borrower—if one of the lenders "falls out" (does not fund its portion of the loan), the borrower is responsible for finding a replacement lender or funding that lender's share of the construction loan.

Construction loan term sheets vary from fairly simple 5–6 pages to 20+ pages that attempt to lay out most of the construction loan agreement provisions. In general, negotiating a construction loan is straightforward, and lenders are fairly predictable in their response to requests to change terms or language, reciting the mantra that "these are our standard terms." Some of the basic terms of a construction loan are described in the following sections.

Loan Amount

The maximum loan amount the lender will be willing to fund will be the lesser of (i) a stated dollar amount, (ii) a maximum percentage of loan to project cost (LTC), (iii) a maximum percentage of loan to the project's as-built stabilized value (LTV) as determined by an appraisal secured by the lender, or (iv) the amount that would yield a minimum debt service coverage ratio (DSCR) or minimum debt yield.[1]

Construction lenders are very conservative in their underwriting, and will critically evaluate the borrower's proposed income and expenses to make certain that the proforma is realistic. Borrower's and their equity partners strive to maximize the loan amount (i.e. pursue higher "leverage") as loan interest rates are low and more leverage creates higher internal rates of return on equity due to the project's internal rate of return being higher than the loan interest rate. Loan officers, on the other hand, realize they are earning a very low rate of return on their loaned funds, making them risk averse. This dynamic tension creates opportunities for extensive dialogue with the lender and its appraiser on why the proforma income and expenses are realistic and obtainable.

Track Record of Developer, Financial Strength, Competitive Projects

Beyond the loan amount and discussions regarding the borrower's proforma, the other major focal points for lenders are strength and track record of the developer and guarantors, and current and proposed competitive projects. If substantial new projects have come into the market recently or are proposed or under construction, the lender will require that the market study evaluate recent absorption (leasing) of the new projects, and forecast out tenant demand through completion of the proposed project.

Although loan term sheets tend to be rather mundane, the key areas of interest to the developer tend to be more business terms versus legal provisions. Loan fees, interest rates, term of the loan (including extension options and extension fees), nonrecourse and recourse guarantees and financial covenants of the guarantors are among the items that are most heavily negotiated.

Guarantees

At the closing of a construction loan, the lender will require that several guaranty agreements be executed by an individual or entity affiliated with the developer who has a significant net worth and liquid assets, as follows.

Non-Recourse Carveout Guaranty

In all cases the construction lender will require that an individual or entity affiliated with the developer, who has a significant net worth and liquid assets, guaranty certain nonrecourse "carveouts" to the loan. Typical items covered by a nonrecourse carveout guaranty (sometimes referred to as the "bad-boy guaranty") are:

- Not applying income from the property to operating expenses and debt payments.
- Misappropriating insurance proceeds.
- Material misrepresentations in securing the loan.
- Fraud or material waste resulting in loss of the property.
- Failure to maintain the loan in balance prior to stabilization.
- Removal of any property from the project that is not replaced with property of similar value.
- Failure to maintain property insurance.
- Any breach of the hazardous materials indemnity.
- Net operating losses through stabilization of the project.

On the net operating loss guaranty, it is *critical* that the obligation of the guarantor terminate after the owner/borrower has tendered possession of the project back to the lender, although the lender may require as a condition to the offer of possession that the borrower secure an updated clean environmental report for the project.

Hazardous Materials Indemnity

Hazardous material indemnities are fairly straightforward and seldom controversial, involving a simple agreement to indemnify the lender against any liability the lender may incur by reason of any adverse environmental conditions on the property.

Completion Guaranty

Similarly, guarantees of completion are also relatively non-controversial. The guarantor basically guarantees all of the loan agreement provisions relating to lien-free completion of the project, and with respect to retail and office projects, also assures all obligations of the borrower to complete tenant finish out. In return, so long as the guarantor is fulfilling its obligations, the lender should agree to make the remaining loan proceeds available to the guarantor subject to the terms of the loan agreement, other than those covenants that are personal to the borrower. The guarantor should petition the lender to allow a reasonable period of time to bring the project back on schedule before the lender is allowed to exercise any of its monetary remedies against the guarantor.

Guaranty of Repayment

As discussed previously, lower loan-to-cost loans normally do not require a guaranty of the loan from the developer. However, if the developer desires to increase the loan-to-cost above 60% or 65%, lenders may then require a guaranty of a portion of the loan. Repayment guarantees normally have "burnoff" provisions, where the guaranty reduces at certain milestones, such as completion of the project, project stabilization and hitting certain debt-service-coverage ratios.

Financing Brokers

Although a larger developer may have an internal chief financial officer or VP of finance with experience in sourcing debt and equity, a smaller developer with a limited track record may face more challenges locating financing. In addition, even larger developers occasionally encounter projects or submarkets where finding debt or equity is challenging. In this case, the developer may turn to one of the financing brokers (such as Holliday Fenoglio Fowler, Northmarq or CBRE). These brokers have extensive relationships with lenders and equity partners and can vastly expand the pool of financing candidates. Broker fees for these services can be expensive but engaging a broker can be highly beneficial if they move a stuck project off dead center. When negotiating their brokerage agreements, it is fairly typical to exclude financing sources that the developer has worked with in the past, or to pay the broker a reduced fee if financing ultimately comes from those sources. In addition, brokerage agreements typically require the payment of fees for future projects with any financing source that was introduced to the developer by the broker, which is appropriate but should be limited in time. Finally, my experience is that financing brokerage agreements are poorly written and are largely drafted to protect the broker and, given the large fees charged by financing brokers, developer's legal counsel should be involved early in reviewing and commenting on these agreements.

Loan Balancing

Construction loans must remain "in balance"—if any line item in the development budget increases, and if there is not either an available contingency reserve that the loan documents allow to be used to fund that increase or line items where the borrower can prove that the cost to complete that item will be less than the remaining balance (such that the excess available funds can be reallocated to cover the overage), the borrower will be required to deposit such excess with the lender to "balance" the loan. Typically a principal of the borrower who executes completion guarantees will also be required to guaranty the funding of any such shortfall.

Alternative Public Financing

To promote certain public purposes, federal, state and local governments may be alternative sources of financing for qualifying projects, by providing loans, grants, tax credits, tax abatements, etc. As with any governmental program, these project subsidies come with regulatory and compliance requirements, application processes and potentially contentious public hearings and required input from local stakeholders. With all forms of public financing described below, engaging a qualified consultant should be the first priority as they can help navigate through the political and regulatory minefields.

New Market Tax Credit Financing

New market tax credits (NMTCs) are federal income tax credits that can be used to attract private investment in real estate projects, community facilities and operating businesses in qualifying distressed communities,[2] thereby creating jobs, providing goods and services or eliminating food deserts. The NMTC program has generated $8 of private investment for every $1 of federal spending, financed over 5,400 businesses, and created 178 million square feet of development. Note that certain projects are not eligible for NMTC financing, such as casinos, golf courses and rental residential properties.

The process begins when a Community Development Entity (CDE) makes an application to the Community Development Financial Institutions Fund (CDFI), a department of the US Treasury, for an allocation of NMTCs. CDEs are normally subsidiaries of banks or are branches or divisions of state or local governments or nonprofit entities formed to make investments in low-income communities.

The NMTCs are then sold by the CDE to investors who receive federal income tax credits equal to 39% of the total qualifying cost of the distressed community project (including the NMTC investor funds and other financing, such as loans, other incentives or owner equity investments), taken over a 7-year period. Recently investors have been paying in the range of $0.80 to $0.85 per $1 of tax benefit received. For example, if the investor pays $0.80 per $1 of credits, and the credits are 39% of the total qualifying project cost, the investor will be providing approximately 31% of the total project cost with the remaining 69% provided by other sources. Although the investor is only providing 31% of the capital, the investor receives the tax credit on the entire project cost, 39 cents in tax credits for a 31-cent investment.

The remaining 69% of the capital for the project is also routed through the CDE in what is called a "leveraged loan" structure, as the entire capital cost must be made by the CDE in order to calculate the NMTCs from the entire project cost. The portion of the project cost from the investor (in our example, 31%) is often funded to the project in the form of "Loan A," while the balance of 69% becomes "Loan B." Loan A is typically a low interest interest-only loan for 7 years, whereas Loan B earns a market rate of interest. Loan A often has a feature where the developer can purchase the loan from the CDE for a nominal amount at the end of the term, resulting in discharge of indebtedness income to the developer. For this reason, many NMTC transactions are developed by for-profit developers for a fee, but owned by not-for-profit entities who are not impacted by the discharged indebtedness.

The transaction chart for a NMTC project is convoluted and can only be understood in the context of tax lawyers driving the structure. Thus, the first action by the developer should be to hire a highly qualified NMTC consultant to provide guidance on structuring the transaction, modeling the proforma and securing an investor.

Low-Income Housing Tax Credits

Back in 1986, Congress dramatically altered the federal tax code, essentially eliminating favorable tax treatment for real estate projects; however, Congress recognized that, without some form of subsidy, future rental residential real estate development would highly favor high rent projects, creating a dearth of affordable housing. The low-income housing tax credit (LIHTC) was added to the 1986 tax act to address the growing need for housing affordable to working class families.

LIHTCs are allocated annually by the Treasury to the various states based on population. Each state then has its own allocating agency that creates parameters under which the state grants the credits to affordable housing projects, but subject to certain minimum standards required by the federal tax code. All LIHTC projects must either rent 20% of the units to people making 50% or less of area median income (AMI) or 40% of the units to people making less than 60% of AMI, with AMIs being adjusted based on presumed family size using 1.5 residents per bedroom (i.e., 1.5 residents in a one-bedroom unit, 3 residents in a two-bedroom unit, 4.5 residents in a three-bedroom unit). In addition, the rents plus utilities for the low-income units must be not more than 30% of household income at those income levels. The easiest means to determine the income, rent and utility levels is by contacting the local public housing authority.

Calculating the LIHTC amount depends on whether the project is financed with tax exempt bonds, in which case the credits are "4% credits," or with other forms of debt financing, which receive "9% credits" Although the 4% credits are fixed at 4%, the so-called 9% credits actually float with interest rates and currently are significantly less than 9%. These 9% credits are secured through a highly competitive process from the state allocating agency based on the "Qualified Allocation Plan" promulgated by the agency, laying out the scoring criteria by which the state will grant the credits. In most states credits requested by affordable housing developers far outstrip the amount of credits available by 6:1 or more. Having a thorough grasp on the state's scoring criteria is critical to securing an allocation, and most tax credit developers submit multiple applications to multiple states to maintain a steady development pipeline.

To determine the amount of credits for the project, the annual tax credit rate (whether the floating 9% credit or the fixed 4% credit) is then applied to the "qualifying basis" of the project (basically the total project cost less certain non-qualifying costs such as land), and that resulting factor is the amount of the tax credits that the project receives each year for 10 years. For instance, in a 4% tax-exempt bond deal if the project qualifying basis is $50 million, and assuming that 100% of the project is rented to qualifying low-income residents, the project receives $2 million per year in tax credits for 10 years, or a total of $20 million in tax credits. The credits are then "sold" to an investor who becomes a limited partner in the project. If the $20 million in tax credits is sold for 80 cents/$1.00, this would generate a $16 million equity investment, and the remaining $34 million in project cost would be financed with tax-exempt bonds, other state or local loans or below-market grants or deferred developer fees. The limited partner uses the tax credits to offset its tax liability. In order for the investor to have the benefit of the tax credits, they must also own substantially all of the economic interest in the project during the 10 year tax credit period, which without other arrangements would not be acceptable to the developer. Tax counsel can assist with structures to flow more of the operating cash flow to the developer, frequently through either asset management fees to the developer or by using a master-lease structure.

Note that LIHTCs can only be earned on units that are rented at affordable rents to low-income residents. If the project has a market rate component, an "applicable fraction" is applied to the potential tax credits—using our example above, if the project is 40% affordable and 60% market, then the $20 million in tax credits would be reduced to only $8 million ($20 million x 40%), and if the credits are sold for 80 cents/$1.00, generating $6.4 million in equity, the remaining $43.4 million of project cost would then need to be funded from other sources. To maximize the amount of equity secured from the LIHTCs, most affordable housing projects are 100% affordable or have only a small portion of market rate units.

LIHTC units must be in compliance—with verified tenant income levels and the correct rent levels—for the entire 10-year credit period and are verified via annual reporting requirements to and periodic audits by the state allocating agencies. Many state allocating agencies will require prospective applicants to agree to maintain longer compliance periods in order to score more "points" in the competitive process for 9% credits or as part of receiving a tax-exempt bond allocation of 4% credits. LIHTC investors typically require the developer to guarantee that the project remain in compliance, mandating the hiring of a management company that has vast experience in managing affordable housing projects. At the end of the credit period, the limited partner's interest in the project is typically subject to a call right, where the developer can buy out the investor's interest for a relatively nominal amount.

LIHTC projects tend to be driven by the tax credits and fee revenue earned by the developer, rather than by operating income or profits from sale of the project, as the rent levels tend to tamp down operating profits and value. Developer fees are outsized compared to market rate rental projects, with most states allowing developer fees in the range of 15–18% of qualifying project costs.

> *A word of caution—be careful of deferring developer fees to close project funding gaps and be wary of chasing what looks like a large developer fee on a project that ultimately operates on a low margin, as paying out on investor and loan guarantees can quickly eat into developer fee revenue.*

Many of the same companies that work with NMTC developers also have consultants who assist LIHTC developers on structuring the transaction, modeling the proforma and securing an investor.

Historic Tax Credits

Substantial rehabilitation costs for buildings listed in the National Register of Historic Places or certified as contributing to the significance of a "registered historic district" qualify for a historic tax credit equal to 20% of the qualifying certified rehabilitation costs. The rehabilitation must be done according to the federal standards for historic rehabilitation to ensure that the historic character of the building is preserved. After the renovation, the building must be used for an income-producing purpose for at least 5 years. Owner occupied residential properties do not qualify for the credit. To meet the substantial rehabilitation test, the rehabilitation costs must exceed the greater of $5,000 or the building's "adjusted basis." Adjusted basis is the purchase price of the building (excluding land cost at the time of purchase), less depreciation previously taken, plus the cost of capital improvements made since purchase. As a practical matter for buildings purchased and immediately renovated, the adjusted basis is the purchase price of the property less the value of the land. If the purchase price of the building excluding land value is $1 million, then $1 million in renovation must occur for the renovation costs to qualify for the historic credit.

Securing the credits involves an application to the National Park Service outlining the renovations, which then reviews the application and certifies that the renovation meets the federal rehabilitation standards.

Once the historic credits have been certified by the National Park Service, renovations can proceed. The developer monetizes the tax credits by one of two structures, which have different economic impact: a single tier structure in which the tax credit investor is admitted to the entity that owns the property or a "master-lease" structure where the developer and its other investors own the property, which is leased to a master tenant in which the tax credit investor is the majority partner, with the owner entity agreeing to pass the tax credits through to the master tenant (and ultimately to the tax credit investor). Generally speaking, the benefit of the master lease structure is that the operating cash flow from the property can be stripped and passed on to the ownership entity through the master lease payments, with the tax credits being allocated to the tax credit investor. There are upsides and downsides to both structures,[3] and a competent tax advisor should assist in structuring the transaction. In any event, historic tax credits typically are sold close to par (100 cents on the dollar) as the credits are earned in the year in which the renovations are complete and certified by the National Park Service.

Opportunity Zones

Opportunity Zones (OZs) are a relatively new federal program, put in place in 2017 to provide tax incentives to investors willing to fund businesses in certain low-income census tracts that have been designated by the governor and approved by the United States Treasury Department. Various mapping tools exist to locate certified OZs.[4]

The tax benefits from investing in OZs are twofold:

- Deferral of Tax on Gains from Sale of Assets: An OZ investor can defer, until the earlier of December 31, 2026 or the date of sale of the OZ investment, any gain incurred on the sale of assets that generated the funds for the OZ investment. The amount of gain that is then includible is the lesser of the original gain deferred or the increase in the fair market value of the OZ investment over the amount of the OZ investment.
- Step-Up in Basis: In addition to the deferral of gain described above, if an OZ investment is held for over 5 years, the basis in the OZ investment is deemed to be increased by 10% of the amount of the deferred gain, and if the OZ investment is held for longer than 7 years the original basis is increased by an added 5% of the amount of the deferred gain. If the OZ investment is held for more than 10 years, only the deferred gain described above is recognized, and none of the increase in value of the OZ investment is subject to tax.

These two tax benefits allow OZ investors to provide capital to projects in lower income communities with lower return rate expectations. Most OZ investors are wealthy individuals who sell appreciated stock, and then invest in an Opportunity Zone Fund, and not directly in an OZ project. Opportunity Zone Funds, which must be certified by the US Treasury Department and must have 90% of their assets invested in OZ projects, aggregate cash from these wealthy investors and then invest in and manage OZ projects.

Unlike NMTCs and LIHTCs, opportunity zone projects are not subject to a competitive process to secure the tax benefits.

Tax Increment Financing

Tax Increment Financing (TIF) is a mechanism used by local governments to incentivize development or redevelopment in neglected areas or areas where investment is favored, such as near mass transit. The local governmental agency defines the district boundaries, sets a base year valuation for all assets within the district and establishes a termination date for the district. The taxes calculated off the base valuation continue to fund overall city services, with the tax on any increase in value above the base being redeployed directly back into the district.

District boundaries are often gerrymandered to accomplish certain policies, such as transit-oriented development TIFs that reduce car dependency by creating mixed-use walkable neighborhoods near transit stations.

Upon forming a TIF district, the city may float tax-exempt bonds backed by the future TIF tax revenue, and use the bond proceeds to make grants or low interest rate loans to proposed projects within the TIF, although most TIF funds must be used for a "public purpose," which is somewhat broadly defined to include such costs as affordable housing, facade improvements, demolition of dilapidated structures, streetscape enhancements, environmental cleanup, etc. As additional projects add tax base to the district, the city may have excess revenue above the bond payments, and may use these additional funds to reinvest in the district.

Each state and local government have different guidelines governing TIF financing, which can be easily discerned by contacting the city's economic development department.

Enterprise Zones

States' Enterprise Zone (EZ) programs provide state tax refunds to encourage job creation and private investment in economically distressed areas. Local governments propose areas within their communities for EZ designation that must be approved by the state, and in exchange for companies making a minimum capital investment and creating a minimum number of jobs (possibly with a minimum required wage amount and with a required percent of the jobs being filled by lower income residents) within the EZ, the state then agrees to rebate a certain portion of the states' taxes back to the business, subject to a capped amount.

Developers of purpose built facilities for companies can negotiate with the companies to apply some or all of the tax rebate be applied to project costs, including tenant finish out that could otherwise be a cost borne by the developer/landlord.

HUD 221(d) Loans

As an alternative to a standard construction loan, multifamily projects (including seniors' independent living apartments) for families, elderly and the handicapped qualify to apply for loans guaranteed by the federal government through the Section 221(d) program. This program insures lenders against loss on mortgage defaults, and permits long-term fixed rate mortgages. HUD 221(d) loans are highly beneficial to the owner, with automatic conversion from a construction loan to a permanent loan upon certain conditions and 40-year amortization periods (versus 30 years for the typical permanent loan). All families are eligible to occupy units whose mortgage is insured under the program, without any income restrictions.

These HUD loans are typically processed by approved lenders through Multifamily Accelerated Processing (MAP). The MAP-approved lender works with the developer to secure all the necessary paperwork for a pre-application. HUD then reviews these materials and will either "invite" the approved lender to apply for a commitment for mortgage insurance, or will decline to consider the application further. The main reasons that HUD declines to insure a mortgage are either too much supply in the market or development costs are excessive.

Combining Sources of Alternative Financing

Development projects that have a social purpose, such as affordable housing or retail or community facilities in underserved markets, may need multiple sources of equity and debt financing, often referred to as a "deep capital stack" or "subsidy layering"—involving developer funds, GP equity, LP equity, construction financing and one or more sources of public subsidy. For instance, a developer may work with a city or a transit agency to create a mixed-use project, with apartments over retail near a transit stop in a lower income community, with parking for residential, retail and transit uses, to encourage walkability and transit use and to provide much needed services. To make this project feasible, the developer, working with its legal counsel and advisors, should determine all sources of potential financing—those that come to mind in our example project include a HUD 221(d)(4) loan, developer equity, LIHTCs, TIF financing, NMTCs and EZ tax rebates.

Unfortunately, not all of these alternative forms of financing play well with each other, as the various federal and state funding programs and each lender and equity partner will have their own requirements, and ultimately the developer must either play by the most restrictive rules of all the financing providers, or find a path around the rules. In addition, knowledgeable creativity in structuring the transaction may result in a substantial increase in one or more subsidy. Using the example above, HUD until recently did not allowed any portion of a 221(d)(4) loan to be used, directly or indirectly, for any costs associated with retail development, even if the retail is condominiumized away from the multifamily and the costs are appropriately segregated, while NMTCs cannot be used to fund residential development. For any project involving subsidy layering the developer should interview a number of local attorneys and financing consultants to determine the professionals with the greatest decree of experience with the anticipated forms of financing.

Notes

1 See page 36 for additional information on lender metrics.
2 Several consulting firms have websites that assist in locating qualifying areas, such as https://www.bakertilly.com/insights/new-markets-tax-credit-and-low-income-housing-tax-credit-mapping-tool and https://www.novoco.com/resource-centers/new-markets-tax-credits/data-tools/nmtc-mapping-tool
3 www.novoco.com/periodicals/articles/qa-single-tier-vs-master-lease-structure
4 www.novoco.com/sites/default/files/mapbox/opzone/gozone_map_19.html

15 Construction Contracts

While debt and equity financing for the project is being secured, the developer should also be securing construction bids, whether internally if the developer has a construction group, or externally from third party contractors. As discussed previously, optimally the developer will approach the project as a design-build exercise, where the contractor and major subcontractors are brought into project design early to reduce costs and promote construction efficiencies. The alternative of "value engineering," bringing the project into budget by choosing lower quality materials, is demoralizing to the development team that has worked toward the project vision for well over a year.

The American Institute of Architects (AIA) has promulgated forms to use in drafting construction contracts. By far the most commonly used contract form is the A102, entitled "Standard Form of Agreement Between Owner and Contractor where the basis of payment is the Cost of the Work Plus a Fee with a Guaranteed Maximum Price." The A102 is paired with the A202, "General Conditions of the Contract for Construction." The A102 basically allows the contractor to charge for the cost of the work plus its profit and overhead, but subject to a maximum price, providing the owner some certainty in planning the development budget. Cost overruns that are within the control of the contractor become the contractor's responsibility, although the owner will still be obligated to cover uncontrollable hidden site conditions, excessive weather delays and other items of force majeure. The General Conditions establishes the more detailed rights, responsibilities, and relationships of the owner, contractor, and architect, whereas the A102 contains the business terms.

A thorough discussion of construction contract provisions and suggested changes is the subject of very technical tomes, and there are lawyers who specialize in only construction contracts and construction litigation. With the AIA drafting the AIA forms, it is not surprising that the forms are not the best legal documents and are very protective of, and provide too much authority to, the architect. For the most part attorneys working with the AIA forms modify the forms to remove the authority of the architect and place those rights with the owner itself.

DOI: 10.1201/9781003264514-15

Key Construction Contract Provisions

Development associates should be aware of certain key provisions that are likely to either be heavily negotiated with the contractor or will be focused on by the GP and LP equity partners:

- **Guaranteed maximum price (GMP) contract**: As the preliminary construction bids come in from the potential contractors, the developer will need to align those bids with the development budget to determine whether the project as bid is financially feasible, i.e., are the debt and equity sources sufficient to cover the development budget, inclusive of the hard construction costs and soft development costs? If not, the developer may then reengage with the contractors with the most viable bids, and ask them to "sharpen their pencils" to reduce their bids in order to win the contract.
- **Construction timeline including unit and amenity deliveries**: Contractors will typically want to back-end the project schedule, providing units as late as possible to avoid liquidated damages. Developers and their equity partners desire units earlier in order to begin earning revenue to offset construction loan interest and begin returning equity to investors, thereby shutting off the meters on their funds and allowing the developer to start earning its Promote. In addition, delivering project amenities (clubhouses, leasing centers, swimming pools and other common areas) prior to the first units is important to the developer and its management company as these amenities are critical marketing tools in leasing units. The developer should carefully lay out an amenity and project unit delivery schedule (sometimes called the "phasing schedule") with the contractor and negotiate for liquidated damages for failure to deliver the various phases within the agreed time frames, noting that the contractor will request (i) a reasonable buffer before liquidated damages begin to accrue, (ii) attempt to avoid or reduce cumulative liquidated damages (where LDs are running cumulatively on multiple phases that are late in delivery), and (iii) that LD's be capped at a certain percentage of the contractor's profit (e.g., 50%).
- **Contractor's overhead**: To provide a disincentive for the contractor to request extensions of time, the contractor's overhead should be capped and additional overhead amounts should not be charged for extended construction time unless due to factors outside the contractor's control.

A word of caution: many of the large contractors will provide construction bids with very low profit and overhead percentages (e.g., 3% vs. 4.5%), and the developer may be tempted to use what appear to be low-cost and very experienced contractors. In this scenario extreme attention should be paid to the definitions of controllable and uncontrollable cost overruns, as large contractors tend to be very adept at documenting and enforcing cost overrun change orders. If a low bid contractor is chosen by the developer with consultation from the LP partner, the joint venture agreement with the LP partner needs to be more lenient on how overrun risk is shared by the LP partner.

Other Construction Related Documents and Processes

- **Staging agreements**: If the project will fill out the development site, such that there is no space for a construction trailer or for offloading or storing of materials, the developer will need to approach adjacent landowners to lease their land for these construction activities.
- **Crane swing easements**: State laws vary on whether an easement is needed to swing a construction crane over the property of an adjoining landowner. For instance, in Georgia an easement is required, but most attorneys in Texas take the position that a crane swing easement is not required, although the easement should be secured if at all possible.
- **Construction access agreements**: If the developer is unable to build the project without entering an adjoining property, a construction access easement will need to be secured from the adjacent landowner.
- **Utility easements and other access rights through adjacent parcels**: If property due diligence investigations reveal that the development site does not have one or more utilities at the edge of the site, discussions with utility company representatives may result in the need to run utility lines through adjacent land parcels. Additionally, as the proposed project is discussed with city planning officials (e.g., during the platting process), the city may require certain access rights from adjacent owners to deal with issues such as cross-access agreements to reduce curb cuts along an adjacent major arterial road or to provide secondary access to the property. In these circumstances easements may need to be secured from one or more adjacent landowners.
- **Notice to proceed**: In order to preserve the lender's first lien position against the property, it is *critically important* that no construction activity of any kind occur on the development site prior to the lender filing its deed of trust or mortgage. In most states any site work prior to the lien filing that is not predevelopment in nature will "prime" the lender's lien, causing the prior work and all subsequent construction work to jump ahead of the lender's lien, making it impossible for the title company to issue first lien lender's coverage to the construction lender. By way of example, a large contractor in Arizona delivered the construction trailer and some construction materials to the site the day before a $350 million loan closing for a grand mixed use project (this was brought to light when the title company performed its pre-closing site inspection later that same day), delaying the closing for 3 weeks and resulting in the title company forcing the contractor, the two developers and their equity partners to spend the next 3 years of construction jumping through administrative hoops. When in doubt, seek local legal counsel's advice before commencing any work

prior to the loan closing. The construction contract should specifically provide that the contractor will not proceed with construction prior to the developer/owner issuing a notice to proceed to the contractor. The notice to proceed should be signed at closing and issued in the following week when the lien filing is confirmed and the contractor and the developer are ready to commence construction.

- **Affidavit of commencement**: After construction commences, to memorialize the date on which construction liens can commence against the property (as versus the prior filing of the construction loan lien), the owner and contractor should sign and record against title an affidavit of commencement.

- **Draw requests, lien releases and downdate endorsements**: On a monthly basis during the course of construction, the contractor will prepare a draw request to the developer, outlining the construction work done during that month and the materials acquired. The developer then uses this construction draw, adding in soft costs such as architect fees, interior design fees, engineering fees and the developer fees, to prepare and submit the full project draw to the owner. The owner, with the architect, then certifies the draw and presents the project draw request to the lender and equity partners. As part of this draw request, the developer also secures "conditional lien releases" from the contractor and all subcontractors and materialmen, releasing any liens against the property for the current month's work, but subject to receiving payment for such work, along with "unconditional lien releases," releasing any liens for prior months (for which payment has already been made). These lien releases are provided to the title company, which then issues a "downdate endorsement," certifying that no new construction liens have been filed against the property since the date of the prior draw.

- **Filed construction liens and bonding over**: During construction, the contractor may dispute the quality or percentage complete of a subcontractor's work or may dispute the quantity or quality of materials provided to the project. If the dispute is not resolved, the subcontractor or materialman may file a lien against the project, which may in turn violate the terms of the construction loan agreement, resulting in the lender refusing to fund that construction draw until the lien filing is removed or "bonded over" by the contractor. The contractor can bond over a lien by securing a bond from a bonding company, typically in an amount equal to 150% of the lien claim. Once the bond is filed of record, the lien claim is removed from the property and instead is deemed to attach to the bond, such that the lien claimant may only then secure satisfaction of its lien claim by pursuing the bond.

- **Certificate of substantial completion**: Upon substantial completion of the project, the owner/developer should request that the project architect memorialize the date of substantial completion and the list of remaining items for final completion (and the agreed time by which the contractor will complete outstanding items) by issuing AIA Form G704. The certificate of substantial completion is typically required by construction lenders to fulfill a loan covenant that completion occur within a set time frame and by equity partners prior to one of the last payments of the developer fee.

- **Affidavit of final completion**: Many states have construction lien filing laws that require that any liens be filed within a certain period after the owner files an affidavit that states a completion date for the project. The owner should timely file this affidavit to cut off all potential lien claims.

16 Management

Approximately 3–4 months prior to opening of a multifamily project, the developer will open a leasing center, either on-site if the contractor has completed the leasing office, in a temporary leasing trailer on-site or in a rented retail or office space near the project. The developer, together with the LP partner, normally vet 3–4 management companies with national stature but solid local presence, and together they select the management company. Although most national management companies will propose using their form of management agreement, developers should require the use of an owner-friendly form of management agreement unless the LP Partner has previously engaged the selected management company on prior projects, in which case the LP Partner will likely require that the management agreement be on their pre-negotiated form.

Management fees are totally negotiable, and are calculated based on the gross receipts from the property excluding "reimbursables"—amounts paid by tenants that the management company is just passing through from outside vendors. A typical fee for a large, Class A apartment complex will be in the range of 2.25–2.75% of monthly gross receipts. The management company is typically paid a minimum fee during lease-up of the project, when project revenue is substantially lower, to cover the overhead costs incurred by the management company, with the minimum fee burning off after the period where the percentage fee applied to the proforma rent projections exceeds the minimum fee, incentivizing the management company to push project lease-up.

In addition to the management fee, the project owner also pays the operating costs of the project and the salaries and leasing fees due to the management and leasing staff employed by the management company and stationed at the property. The management company should be required to operate the project pursuant to a negotiated operating budget and, except for emergency situations, should not, without owner approval, be allowed to incur property obligations outside of a set variance from individual line items in the budget.

> *Developers often view their work ending upon project completion and opening; however, all development efforts can be meaningless if the project is not professionally asset managed to maximize profit, with strong oversight from the development team.*

DOI: 10.1201/9781003264514-16

Before leasing commences, the owner and the regional property manager should establish a leasing and marketing plan: lease rates for each unit type, including premiums for units with views and on higher floors; fees charged for storage units and parking spaces; allowable leasing incentives such as free rent or gift cards; other added charges that are prevalent in the market; anticipated leasing velocity; etc. The owner and manager should also periodically reevaluate which units within the building are leasing faster or slower, and adjust rental rates and leasing incentives appropriately to maximize leasing velocity of all unit types and optimize project profitability during lease-up.

Early leasing of the project causes the project to outperform its proforma, providing better returns to the GP and LP Partners and allows the developer to "get into its Promote" earlier. Leasing bonuses incentivize the leasing staff to lease-up the project rapidly, but only above certain minimum lease rates and only with certain leasing incentives (e.g., free rent and gift cards). Thoughtful owners and managers also closely monitor lease expiration dates, purposely staggering lease terms such that a maximum percentage of leases expire in any given month so that leasing staff is not stressed to secure large volumes of new leases (or lease renewals) in any one period, evening out project cash flow and limiting the number of vacant units that need to be turned/made-ready for re-leasing within any one calendar month.

The management agreement should provide that the manager, assistant manager, head leasing agent and head of maintenance may be interviewed by the owner and the ultimate selection of these project employees (and any replacement thereof) should require the approval of the owner.

Management agreements are always terminable without cause on not less than either 30 or 60 days' notice to the management company, although there may be an initial 6- or 9-month period during which the management company may not be terminated without cause, including failure to reach certain leasing milestones. In general, the owner should have constant dialogue with the management company regarding any failure to attain targeted leasing velocity and project proforma net income, whether due to slow leasing or excessive project expenses.

Annually around the end of October the property management company prepares the project operational budget for the next year and submits the proposed budget to the owner for approval. The owner in turn creates a budget for ownership, including costs of managing the ownership entities, required loan payments and estimated cash flow distributions, and submits the ownership budget to the GP and LP Partners for their approval.

17 Mixed-Use Projects

As discussed in the chapter on pursuits, working on a mixed-use project is an adrenaline rush for developers. When all the components complement each other, creating a sense that the project has its own identity/brand, each of the elements may garner higher rent, be more desirable to tenants and ultimately be more profitable, both operationally and in securing a greater sales price or refinancing amount.

> *The complexity of a mixed-use project can be intoxicating, but they also involve a much greater risk of execution and market timing.*

Mixed-use projects ("MXUs") come in two basic forms—horizontal mixed use, where the uses are not stacked on top of each other but are simply part of a master planned project that shares infrastructure, and vertical mixed use, where uses are stacked and infrastructure is also shared. In either scenario, an MXU project with multiple developers requires an extremely high level of cooperation among the parties, and care should be taken in picking development partners who have amenable personalities and who value collaboration over combat, as hundreds of decisions will need coordination throughout the development process.

Horizontal Mixed-Use Projects

If land is less expensive and abundant, a project with multiple uses can be laid out horizontally, with separate pad sites for multifamily, retail, office, hotel, theater, etc., all with their own parking, but sharing roads, landscaping, signage and utility lines. In this case, the documentation is fairly straightforward, with each developer owning its own site but subject to a "Covenants, Conditions and Restrictions" (referred to in shorthand as "CCRs"), that cover all of the project parcels, and provide for sharing in the cost of developing, constructing and operating the common areas and infrastructure serving the entire mixed-use project. As part of this arrangement, one of the developers typically serves as the master developer of the common areas and infrastructure, sharing the plans for the common improvements with the other developers and their architects and engineers,

DOI: 10.1201/9781003264514-17

securing their input and approval. To ensure that each developer pays its share of the common area development and construction costs, the master developer (and the various lenders and equity partners to the multiple developers) may require that each developer escrow its share of these costs up front, or post a letter of credit backstopping its contribution obligations.

Vertical Mixed-Use Projects

A complete discourse on the details of vertical mixed-use projects could easily fill hundreds of pages. The stacking of uses creates a myriad of interrelationships between the various developers and their equity and lending partners, all of which will want their needs and desires met. As with horizontal MXU projects, one developer typically serves as the lead developer for any shared infrastructure and the "podium" (e.g., shared lobby spaces, shared underground or above-ground parking), and the role of lead developer will largely be navigating the various parties' conflicting desires. Without overgeneralizing, developers tend to be somewhat bombastic individualists, and encouraging many egos to work cohesively requires patience, persistence and a huge amount of diplomatic talent.

Vertical mixed-use projects are best described and learnt in the context of immersion in an actual project, so let's frame the discussion in the context of a hypothetical development project:

- 10 acres of land.
- 120-room hotel.
- 250,000 sq. ft. office building.
- 200-unit multifamily building with below ground parking for the hotel, a ground floor apartment lobby and 20,000 square feet of retail, four floors of above-ground parking for the office tenants and three subsequent floors of apartment parking, with the actual multifamily units sitting above the parking podium.
- Common shared streets and sidewalks, landscaping, art and signage.

Condominium Regime

With stacked vertical spaces owned or used by different parties, and shared common spaces, a condominium regime will need to be imposed to create the separate "airspace parcels," to provide for sharing in operational costs and to establish a condominium association and condo board that will maintain and make decisions regarding the common areas. Although the Uniform Condominium Act has been adopted in most states, each state has its own variations and, to further complicate matters, some major cities (e.g., Los Angeles, Chicago, New York) allow separation of vertical spaces using airspace parcel maps instead of condominium regimes, oftentimes to avoid cumbersome regulatory reviews required of any filed condominium plan. Experienced condo counsel should be engaged early in the planning process to navigate these complexities, and time should be built into the development schedule to tailor the condo documents, allowing leeway for subsequent comments from and revisions required by lenders and equity partners. Condo documents tend to be voluminous, covering a host of issues in great detail, including the following items:

- **Creation of condo units**: The various condo units are described and labeled, typically via an attached set of floor plan drawings. In some states, these drawings are filed of record and may be referred to as a "condo map." Condo drawings/maps are very detailed, calling out separately owned property used solely by one of the owners; limited common areas used by more than one but not all owners; and general common areas used by all the owners. Each floor of each building should be closely examined for hours in a joint session with all the owners, the architects and civil engineers to find and label corridors, utility vaults, utility chases, elevator lobbies and shafts, air return ducts and other facilities used by more than one owner. After the initial draft of the condo drawings/map is prepared, several follow up owner sessions should be scheduled to review and refine the drawings, continuing to peel back the complexities of the condominium structure.
- **Architectural control**: The condominium declaration will provide that the owners must build their initial projects pursuant to approved plans, that external materials and color schemes may only be changed with the approval of the board of the condo association, and that any reconstruction will only be pursuant to plans approved by the condo association. Alternatively, the owners may cede architectural approval to the master project architect to assure that any revisions are in keeping with the overall original design theme.
- **Shared parking; column grids and spacing**: When multiple uses share a common garage, a number of details need to be addressed. How will the cost of the garage be shared among the parties, and what collateral or guarantees will be offered by the other owners/developers to cover their share of the garage costs, providing assurance that each owner/developer will pays its share? Office, retail and hotel parking spaces tend to be wider than multifamily spaces, such that concrete column grids are wider, causing each parking space to be more expensive and can result in the apartment building column spacing (if the multifamily is built above the garage) intruding into the apartment living spaces, creating inconvenient columns in the middle of living rooms and bedrooms, forcing the multifamily owner to develop larger, more costly units to generate the same amount of net rentable area. If a grocery store is located on the ground floor of the multifamily building, to facilitate clear aisles grocery store operators require a minimum amount of columns and carefully placed utility chases. The alternative to both of these design dilemmas is to insert a "transfer deck" above the top garage level (or above the grocery store)—in essence a 4–6-foot-high separate floor that contains a substantial concrete structure to transfer from a tighter column grid to a wider column grid and ganging together utility

chases to reduce the number of chases running through the ground floor uses. In this circumstance, the various owners need to discuss who should pay for the transfer deck.

- **Condo association**: The general and limited common areas, although a component of the individual owners' condominium units, are normally managed by a condo association where each owner is a member, the association has officers and specific voting rights are outlined. Voting rights need to be equitably allocated among the owners, with no one owner having the right to control the actions of the association, but balanced with the ability of an owner to have a significant voice in the operation and maintenance of limited common areas that mainly affect that owner.
- **Sharing in common area costs**: Determining the sharing ratios for common area repair and maintenance is more art than science, arrived at after considerable negotiation between the owners. As to each common area, who uses that facility and what is a fair allocation of costs based on usage? When the usage of parking spaces or other shared facilities can be measured, such as by a sophisticated parking management system, the parties may agree to initially set sharing ratios that are reevaluated on an annual basis based on actual usage data. If loading docks and trash/recycling docks are shared, the owners may employ a dock master to handle scheduling and cleaning, and the dockmaster logs may then be used to periodically recalculate sharing ratios. A spreadsheet listing all of the common areas, which owner is responsible for maintaining each common area and the agreed sharing ratios is typically one of the exhibits to the initial condominium documents.
- **Ancillary revenue**: Complex mixed-use projects can create ancillary income that is not really attributable to any one owner, such as public parking, building billboard signage and fees for use of outdoor common areas. This revenue is oftentimes used to offset general common area expenses. The owners should decide how this unattributable income should be shared.
- **Sharing construction lender**: Although each developer/owner may use a separate construction lender for its part of the project, having multiple lenders creates the need for intercreditor agreements and concerns over lien priority issues (the lien from one of the owner's construction crossing over and encumbering the other owners' properties). In the best-case scenario all of the developer/owners agree to use the same construction lender, albeit with separate loans to each owner for their part of the project. Although having a shared construction lender does not eliminate these problems, this arrangement does result in dealing with only one lender and one lender's counsel versus being in the position of navigating these issues with multiple parties.
- **Sharing master architect, master civil engineer and master contractor**: In a vertically stacked mixed-use project or a project where uses share a common platform, the intense level of coordination required among multiple architects, civil engineers and contractors, all working within a confined space, where the various owners' design drawings must align and construction

carefully sequenced, is akin to watching a finely choreographed dance. Adding more parties to the action only enhances the potential for gaps in drawings or construction, and when something goes wrong, each professional pointing fingers at each other. Although the owners may each employ their own architect, one of the architects needs to act as the coordinating architect, responsible for integrating the plans. One civil engineer should be chosen by all the owners, as segregating this scope of work is impractical, and most of the utilities will be shared and enter the master project at common points. Any building that shares a platform or where uses are stacked should have one contractor that builds the core and shell of the building, while allowing for each owner to hire a separate contractor to finish out the interiors of its condo unit.

- **Shared facilities**: Particularly between hotel and apartment uses, or between office and apartments uses, the owners may determine to create certain shared amenities in lieu of creating separate amenities, such as workout facilities, pools and spas. The owners may share in the cost of building and maintaining these amenities, or may just allow access to such facilities on a fee per use or membership basis.

- **Construction cranes**: Construction cranes are incredibly expensive (for taller buildings, up to a million dollars per crane per year), and each owner can save money by sharing cranes if feasible. For instance, an individual large building may need two cranes, but two adjacent buildings of similar size may be able to share a carefully placed middle crane, thereby having the two buildings needing only three versus four cranes.

- **Construction interruption and shifted costs**: In any vertically stacked mixed-use project, if one of the owners stops the construction of its building certain "shifted costs" will cause the remaining owner(s) to pay for some costs that would otherwise have been paid by the terminating owner. An example would be where contractor overhead that was shared by two owners is now being wholly borne by the remaining owner or the cost of the shared construction crane must now be paid by only the remaining owner. The owners should identify these shifted costs and document that the terminating owner must indemnify the other owners for any shifted costs. In addition, the remaining owners may need rights of access to the terminating owner's condominium unit in order to complete construction of the remaining portions of their individual projects.

- **Noise and odors**: Ground floor bar and restaurant spaces with outdoor patios can result in higher noise levels, which is of particular concern when residential units are located on upper floors. Although higher than normal noise levels are part of urban high rise living, and these people gathering spaces are part of the buzz and excitement of mixed-use projects, attention should be paid to creating a standard for acceptable noise levels and times. In addition, restaurant grease scrubbers and kitchen ventilation should be carefully placed to reduce odors migrating into adjacent retail space or residential units.

- **Vacant ground floor uses**: Vacant ground floor retail space can be very detrimental to a mixed-use project as walkability and ground level aesthetics are highly important to the urban environment. To the extent that ground floor space becomes vacant, the manner of "boarding up" the space, with high design graphics promoting the master project, is critical to minimizing this negative impact.
- **Permitted uses**: The condo documents should restrict retail uses that detract from the overall project. Typically noxious uses such as head shops, liquor stores and massage parlors are prohibited, and certain high parking uses, such as bingo halls or churches may not be allowed. Finally, certain activities may be restricted, such as window signage, sidewalk sales and going out of business sales, to preserve a higher quality aesthetic to the retail environment.
- **Dispute resolution**: Prior to any owner filing a lawsuit against the condominium association, the aggrieved owner and the condo board should be required to have a meeting to attempt to informally resolve the dispute.

A Complex Mixed-Use Example

Grasping the immense amount of details involved in a major mixed-use project is best understood by reviewing a real project.

In 2005 I returned to law firm practice after working as an affordable housing developer for 11 years, and was informed that my timing was perfect as one of the law firm's hotel developer clients was working on a big project in Hollywood. The firm needed an experienced attorney without any clients to work solely on this project for 2½ years. The project was the W Hotel and W Residences (for-sale condominiums) and Legacy Apartments on 6.2 acres at the iconic intersection of Hollywood and Vine (where the Walk of Fame Stars turn the corner), a $620 million co-development between our client, Gatehouse Capital,

Figure 17.1 W Hollywood Hotel and Residences

and Legacy Partners, a large apartment developer out of California. At the time the W Hollywood project was the largest private development project in California. Gatehouse and Legacy secured the rights to develop the site by replying to a "request for proposal" from the community redevelopment authority of Los Angeles County.

The project involved the following:

- 300+ apartment units developed by Legacy Partners (20% of which were affordable) and ground floor retail including a Trader Joe's Grocery Store, financed with equity from CALPERS, low income housing tax credits and tax-exempt bond financing.
- 305-room W Hotel, with 20,000 sq. ft. of ground floor retail including a signature chef restaurant, 143 condominium units and a Victor Drai rooftop nightclub (incorporating the hotel pool after hours) developed by Gatehouse Capital with equity from HEI Hotels & Resorts and EB-5 capital from China used to finance the finish-out of the interior of the nightclub and restaurant.
- Underground parking for all uses in "layers"—with B5 hotel valet parking, B3 and B4 for apartment parking, B2 for condo residential parking and B1 for shared retail parking.
- The apartment project, hotel and residential units are all built above the shared parking podium, valet motor court and ramps to the underground parking garages.
- The entire project shares loading docks and a trash/recycling area.

To subdivide the property into separately owned units, in most states we would create a master "commercial" condominium regime, thereby separating out the hotel, apartments and for-sale residential condominiums (the "Commercial Units"), and then we would impose a subordinate residential condominium regime on the residential condominium unit to create the separate for-sale residences (the "Residential Units"). However, in California, any condominium regime (commercial or residential) must be approved by the state Department of Real Estate, which is a lengthy and cumbersome process. The solution was to create "airspace parcels"—in essence 3D surveys of the proposed Commercial Units, with length, width and height measured above sea level, which are ultimately assembled into a tract map. This architectural drawing process is very detailed. For instance, the hotel/residential condominium building is structured with the hotel lobby bar and hotel restaurant on the first floor protruding into and under the condominium tower but with a separate condo lobby and elevators on the first floor serving the residential condominium tower. The resulting tract map looks like 3D jigsaw puzzle pieces that all fit together, with each puzzle piece being labeled as belonging to the hotel, the residential condominium, the apartments, general common areas or limited common areas.

As mentioned above, the apartment and retail below the apartments (including the grocery store) were owned by Legacy, with the hotel and ground floor retail owned by one entity controlled by Gatehouse and the residential condominium building owned by another Gatehouse controlled entity. To create the legal relationships between the various parcels and owners, the following documents were employed:

- **Covenants, conditions and restrictions (CCRs) for hotel, residential condominiums and apartments** ("Master CCRs"): In a state that is more regulatory friendly toward commercial condominium regimes, a master condominium declaration would be used.
- **Covenants, conditions and restrictions for hotel and residential condominiums** ("Hotel/Condo CCRs"): Governing the relationship between these two owners. Note that even though this document was initially between two Gatehouse controlled entities (such that it appears at the outset to be unnecessary), after the residential condominiums were sold to end users/owners, the condominium association owned the residential condominium entity.
- **Residential condominium declaration**.
- **Condo association governing documents**.
- **Development, cooperation and funding agreement**: Outlining the acquisition of the outparcels, platform design, airspace parcelization, platform design costs (architects, structural engineers, civil engineers) and other common shared expenses. Prior to closing of the construction loan and development equity, the two developers had amassed predevelopment costs in excess of $10 million, and this document outlined the parties' obligations to contribute to these costs.

Among a myriad of additional factors that compounded complexity on the W Hollywood project were:

- **Retail, restaurant and nightclub leases**: The restaurant, retail and nightclub spaces were all owned by the hotel owner and leased to separate owner/operators. The nightclub owner was a joint venture between the hotel owner and the nightclub operator. The grocery store and other retail space below the apartments were owned by the apartment owner, and were leased to retail tenants. All of the retail leases provided that the tenants paid triple net lease payments (rent plus taxes, insurance and other common expenses), including any common area expenses allocated to the retail arising under either the Master CCRs or Hotel/Condo CCRs.
- **Grocery store issues**: Grocery store operators are notoriously well known for being tough negotiators, and for taking an extraordinary amount of time to sign a lease letter of intent and to actually execute the lease. Although grocery stores tend to draw positive attention to mixed-use projects, and to add value (i.e., additional rent) to the other components of the mixed-use project, rents for grocery store tenants do not normally fully support the cost of developing the grocery store space, including extensive parking needed for their customers, such that the rent and profits from other project components must

subsidize the grocery store. The loading dock ramp and dock heights for the project had to be designed to accept tractor trailer trucks delivering supplies to the grocery store under the apartment building.

- **Affordable housing finance**: Initially Legacy planned to use conventional equity financing for the apartment development. However, once they factored in the reduced rent required on the affordable units, additional equity subsidy was needed beyond what CALPERS was willing to fund. At the 11th hour, Legacy added in low-income tax credit (LIHTC) financing with tax-exempt bonds, and negotiating with the LIHTC investor and the bond issuing authorities delayed project commencement by 6 months.
- **Land ownership**: Most of the land for the project was owned by the Metropolitan Transit Authority (MTA) (the project is built around the Hollywood and Vine subway stop). However, 7 outparcels had to be acquired to assemble the entire site. Once acquired, these parcels were donated by the developers to the MTA. The MTA's initial requirement was that all of the land then be ground leased to the developers, but we quickly determined that for-sale residential condo units can only be built on fee owned land, such that the hotel and apartment parcels were ground leased, with the residential condo unit land being deeded outright to that owner.
- **Nightclub**: The nightclub, sitting on the roof of the hotel and adjacent to the condominium tower, with its loud music and use of the outdoor rooftop hotel pool, created some unique design and operational issues. To attempt to mitigate transmission of bass music notes through the hotel skin, the nightclub floor was actually suspended or floated from support beams and did not directly abut the ceiling of the top floor of the hotel. The lease for the nightclub contained strict noise standards after certain hours.

Working on a complex mixed-use project with multiple developers, owners, tenants and debt and equity partners is an exciting and emotional experience that will likely be the pinnacle of your career. The details are all-consuming and fitting the jigsaw puzzle pieces into a cohesive pattern, closing the transaction, watching it under construction and attending the grand opening will be the greatest learning experience you ever encounter. The end result is incredibly rewarding, but also demands almost 24/7 work for a number of years.

18 Refinancing

Refinancing a project is very similar to closing a construction loan, but without the need to delve into construction details and proforma operating income and expenses. Construction costs have been incurred, construction is complete, and rents and expenses are largely determined, simplifying the lender's underwriting of the project. Because construction and rent-up risk have been removed from the risk profile, permanent loans are funded at lower interest rates and with higher loan-to-value than construction loans, allowing the equity partners in the owner (developer, GP Partner and LP Partner) to "take money off the table," reducing their investment, increasing their leverage and their rate of return. For the developer, returning capital will bring the developer closer to earning its Promote. A permanent loan is normally pursued once the property has stabilized net operating income sufficient to support a $1.1\times$ or $1.2\times$ debt service coverage ratio. In addition, loan sizing will be constrained by the ratio of the loan to actual appraised value (LTV), with the maximum loan amount being in the range of 70–75% LTV.

In preparing to refinance the project, the developer should attend to the following items:

- **Affidavit of completion**: The architect should do a final inspection and execute an affidavit of final completion indicating that the project has been completed by the contractor substantially in accordance with the plans and specifications.
- **Title**: All construction liens should be cured (or bonded over) and the owner's title policy should be brought current showing no liens against the property. A title commitment for the permanent lender should be ordered showing the proposed lender as insured and also showing no liens or other encumbrances against the property, other than easements that benefit the property or are outside the project building's foundations.
- **As-built survey**: As the project nears substantial completion, the surveyor should be asked to prepare an as-built survey showing the actual locations of buildings, sidewalks, easements and other on-the-ground conditions, all of which should be within the site boundaries and city set-backs or in appropriate easements.

DOI: 10.1201/9781003264514-18

- **Property condition**: The chosen refinancing lender will requisition a property condition report (PCR) to determine if any portion of the construction needs to be remedied. The most frequently experienced deficiency is failure to properly secure the structures against water intrusion. All flashing and other water intrusion protection measures should be carefully monitored during construction and should be reevaluated as the owner prepares to refinance the construction loan. Prior to pursuing possible lenders, the developer should secure its own third-party inspection report, and then remedy any deficiency conditions that are cited. To the extent that any deficiencies identified in the PCR are not repaired when the permanent loan closes, the lender will likely require an oversized escrow of funds to be held pending completion of the repairs.
- **Updated environmental report**: The developer should ask the loan officer for a list of lender-approved environmental companies, and the developer should then secure a post-completion environmental Phase I report naming the owner and the lender as parties entitled to rely on the report.
- **Appraisal**: The lender will commission an appraisal of the project to determine the LTV. Appraisers tend to be very conservative in determining operating expenses, oftentimes using, on a line-item by line-item basis, the higher of their estimates of each budget line item or the actual expenses incurred by the project. In order to secure the largest possible loan amount, the developer, with assistance from the property management company, should be prepared to have a dialogue with the appraiser and loan officer to challenge assumptions that the developer considers unreasonable.

The permanent loan closing process is otherwise largely similar to closing the construction loan, focusing on providing due diligence information to the lender.

19 Selling the Project

After the project is completed and approaching full occupancy, the developer, along with its GP and LP partners, will need to decide to either sell the project or hold the project long-term. As mentioned above, the LP Partner's investment horizon may be longer term, whereas the developer may be more interested in selling the property and realizing its full Promote profit. If the developer determines to exit the project, the developer may simply sell its interest in the Project to the LP Partner (and the GP Partner may "tag along" and sell its interest as well), either pursuant to a pre-negotiated forced sale right or simply through opening negotiations with the LP Partner. Alternatively, all parties to the owner may decide to sell and engage a broker to market and sell the property.

The developer and LP Partner will normally interview 3–5 reputable brokerage companies who vie for the right to sell the Project. The brokers will tout their experience in recently selling similar projects in the area and the stable of buyers they have worked with in the past. The owner should be interested not just in the company's experience, but focus on the expertise of the particular team of brokers who will lead the marketing efforts. Although the owner should request input on a potential sales price for the project, the owner should not lock into the broker offering the most optimistic projected sales price, asking pointed questions after having done its own analysis of recent sales transactions.

Once the broker is engaged, their marketing department prepares a pitch book outlining the specific attributes of the project: project description and amenities; location; surrounding area; demographics of the city and the submarket; project rents and operating expenses; rents from comparable properties; etc. A professional photographer will prepare a portfolio to include in the marketing brochure, and recently the larger broker companies are preparing high quality 3–5-minute videos of projects, complete with drone footage. With highly sought-after assets, the pitch book may also contain the proposed form of purchase and sale agreement, and each bidder is asked to provide comments to the contract when they submit their bids.

The broker will then distribute the marketing materials to its database of potential purchasers and set a due date for bids. Prospective purchasers submit their bids, typically in the form of a short, nonbinding letter of intent outlining critical terms. After the bid deadline, the broker and owner will open the

DOI: 10.1201/9781003264514-19

bids and create a summary of the details of the various offers, focusing mainly on the bidders' background, offer price, amount of earnest money deposits and when they become nonrefundable, inspection period, closing timeframes and conditions to closing. In most asset sales, the initial earnest money is relatively large (e.g., $500,000–1,500,000 on a $50 million sales price) and oftentimes after the inspection period, when the initial earnest money is no longer refundable (referred to as "goes hard"), the buyer will be required to post additional hard earnest money. If the bids come in lower than the amount the developer and its equity partners believe is attainable, the seller may return to the bidders and request that they provide "best and final" bids.

Once the sale has been awarded to a bidder, the owner and the purchaser negotiate the purchase contract, which normally must be executed within 30–45 days or the seller may move on to the next most desirable bidder. In broad terms, project sale contracts are not highly negotiated documents, as the number of controversial terms is relatively limited, although some large institutional buyers tend to delve into the more minor details.

After the buyer has an opportunity to inspect the property, the buyer delivers a Property Condition Report (PCR) to the owner, along with a letter from the buyer outlining those items that the buyer either wants to be remedied or receive a credit (reduction in the purchase price) at the closing. This list is frequently the most heavily contested aspect of selling a project, and can feel at times like the requested remedial measures amount to an opportunity for the buyer to retrade the sales price.

Project service agreements are provided by the seller to the buyer as part of the due diligence items delivered under the purchase contract. During the inspection period the buyer provides the seller with a list of those agreements that the buyer wants to assume versus those that the buyer desires be terminated.

The actual closing of an asset sale involves detailed accounting for income and expense prorations between the parties (with the management company's assistance), where the seller gets credit for or charged for items attributable to the days before the closing date and the buyer gets credit for or charged for items attributable to the closing date and thereafter. For instance, assume in a 30–day month that rent is due on the first of the month and the closing occurs on the 14th of the month. As to rent and other income items collected by the seller attributable to the month of closing, the seller would give the buyer a credit (reduction in the purchase price) for rent attributable to the 15th through the 30th. Similarly, as to expenses that have already been paid by the seller that cover the entire month, the purchase price would in essence be increased by the expenses attributable to the period from the 15th through the 30th of the month. This process is further complicated when rent has been collected from some but not all of the tenants for the month of closing. In this case, there is typically a true-up between the buyer and seller 90–120 days post-closing, with rent collected by the buyer after the closing first being attributable to any rent due the buyer (for the post-closing period) before any rent is then used to pay the seller for periods prior to the closing. Expense items that should be considered include bonus and vacation accruals for leasing and management staff; property taxes; gift cards, free rent and other incentives given to tenants; and prepaid quarterly or annual service contracts. Overall, closing prorations involve heavy lifting from the accounting staff (or the analysts) reviewing each income and expense item to determine the appropriate allocations to pre- and post-closing time periods.

Shortly after the inspection period expires, the accounting department, analyst or development associate should prepare a spreadsheet identifying all the prorations, secure input on the spreadsheet from the management company and the title closing officer, and begin to secure the data to complete the prorations. The spreadsheet (and accompanying title closing statement) will then need to be updated as the week of closing arrives. To avoid last minute scrambling to bring the numbers current to the date of closing, it can be helpful to pick a proration date 4–5 days prior to the closing date, and then 60–90 days after closing bring the numbers current through the closing date as part of the post-closing true-up.

20 Retail and Office Leasing

Unlike residential rental developments, retail and office projects involve pre-leasing requirements of larger blocks of space. Although having a greater percentage of the project preleased reduces the risk for the borrower, tenants who sign up prior to construction commencement realize that the developer needs preleasing for the project to commence, and will negotiate terms (rents, tenant finish-out and leasing concessions) less favorable to the developer. Once the project exterior construction is complete, and preleasing by prime tenants has occurred, later smaller retail or office tenants tend to pay higher rates. This leads to a dynamic tension for the developer—leasing more early reduces risk, but may lower overall economic returns by sacrificing the higher effective rents that can be negotiated later in the development cycle.

Retail and commercial leases contain provisions that are foreign to apartment tenancies but are critical to the operation and financial performance of commercial projects, including the following:

- **Net leases**: Typically, commercial leases are "triple net," meaning that in addition to base monthly rent the tenant pays property taxes, insurance and common area maintenance (CAM). As this arrangement provides less certainty to the tenant on total lease payments, landlord and tenant set a base year one CAM charge, and agree that annual increases will be subject to a cap (e.g., CPI based or a maximum percentage per year). Taxes and insurance are uncontrollable costs, and are not normally subject to a cap.
- **Premises size**: The tenant pays for rentable square feet but can only use "usable square feet." There are typically no exclusions for columns, recessed entries and the like. Rentable square feet is usable square feet plus a common area factor based on the tenant's pro rata share of common areas within the building. If a building has 100,000 sq. ft. but only 90,000 sq. ft. of usable space, the common area factor is determined by the ratio of 100,000/90,000, or 1.11. If a tenant within the building has 20,000 sq. ft. of usable space, the rental sq. ft. is 20,000 × 1.11 or 22,200 sq. ft, and that tenant then pays rent based on 22,200 sq. ft.
- **Parking**: Is parking reserved and if not are there an adequate number of conveniently located total parking spaces within the building to service the

DOI: 10.1201/9781003264514-20

tenant's use, given the other tenants' uses? Will parking be paid for by the tenant or its customers or is parking part of base rent?

- **Tenant finish out**: The lease should specify what work the landlord performs versus the finish out that the tenant will complete. Most commercial landlords provide the tenant with a tenant improvement (TI) allowance to pay for or subsidize the tenant's finish out of its leased space in exchange for an increased amount of rent to cover these up-front funds provided by the landlord, referred to as the landlord's "amortization" of these costs over the life of the lease. TI allowances required by initial lease-up of the project should be included in the original proforma, and TI allowances needed to release space should be part of the operating proforma in subsequent years. To the extent that the tenant does not use all of the TI allowance for physical improvements, the lease should state whether the tenant can apply the unused balance to other costs of entering into the tenancy, such as moving costs, furniture, fixtures and equipment, or soft costs (such as architect and engineering fees).
- **Heating, ventilation and air conditioning (HVAC) equipment**: In retail buildings, the tenant installs all HVAC equipment using its TI allowance, although roof penetrations are reviewed by the landlord. In office buildings, HVAC is provided at a common point on each floor, and only the runs from the central location to the tenant's space are installed by the tenant, and HVAC utility costs are built into the base rent or are part of the CAM charges.
- **Guarantees**: For tenants without a significant credit history/rating, the landlord will require a lease guarantor, at least for an initial period of the lease term.
- **Expansion space**: Frequently a major tenant in an office building will request certain rights with respect to adjacent expansion space within the building. For instance, the tenant may be leasing part of Floor 11, with the balance of the floor being presently unleased, and the tenant may negotiate for a right of first offer (ROFO) or right of first refusal (ROFR) on the adjacent space. With a ROFO, if the landlord desires to start leasing the adjacent space, the landlord is required to first inform the tenant of the terms under which the landlord would be willing to enter into a lease, and the tenant then has a certain period to accept or reject the offered terms. If the tenant rejects the terms, the landlord can only lease the space to third parties on those terms or other terms that are more beneficial to the landlord (costlier to the new tenant). With a ROFR, the landlord can enter into negotiations with prospective tenants for the space, but upon receiving a term sheet from a new tenant, the landlord must present that offer to the current tenant, who will have a set period of time to match those terms or relinquish the ROFR. For obvious reasons landlords desire a ROFO versus a ROFR, as negotiating new tenant lease terms can be time consuming and with a ROFR the existing tenant can then thwart the landlord's efforts and harm the relationship with the new tenant by exercising the ROFR.

21 Retail Development

Even before the COVID crisis, the United States was vastly over-retailed, having almost 7–10 times the amount of retail space per person than European countries, and online stores continue to eat into bricks-and-mortar retail sales. Tens of thousands of retail stores and restaurants are likely to close because of the recent COVID-19 pandemic. In a post-COVID online shopping world, retail developers have become very focused on restaurant and service retail tenants, as socialization with friends and hair/nail/spa, tutoring and medical services must all occur in person. Despite the bleak overall retail outlook, new housing developments have continued through the crisis, and the pent-up demand for single family homes and apartments will drive the development of new retail projects near new housing formations.

Due to debt and equity requirements and the needs of retail and restaurant tenants, successful retail projects are planned around the following criteria.

Prime Retail Locations

Drive-through restaurants, strip retail centers and grocery stores are normally located on the path home from work and not along the path to work, to allow customers to avoid left turns across multiple lanes of traffic. Most city planning departments will require a traffic study to determine if roadway infrastructure enhancements, such as turn lanes, deceleration lanes or traffic signals are needed. Early in the development process the retail developer should meet with the engineering or traffic department of the city to determine if the developer will be required to pay for or incorporate any traffic safety enhancements.

Retail Rent Structure

Rent payable by retail tenants can be structured in two manners: fixed monthly rent or minimum monthly rent with percentage rent. With percentage rent, the tenant pays a minimum monthly payment plus a percentage of gross sales above a floor. By way of example, if the fixed rent is $5,000 per month, the tenant may be required to pay 5% of monthly sales above $100,000 (referred to

DOI: 10.1201/9781003264514-21

as the "breakpoint"). With both fixed rent and percentage rent leases, a triple net (NNN) lease should be employed, with the tenants paying their pro rata shares of the shopping center's taxes, insurance and common area operating expenses (CAM). From the developer's perspective, the definition of allowable CAM expenses should be expansive, including periodic remodeling expenses, although larger retail tenants will likely negotiate to remove capital costs from CAM allocations.

Lead tenants such as grocery stores or big box retailers may demand a lower base rent than would otherwise be acceptable to the developer, but in exchange may be willing to accept a lower breakpoint after which percentage rent begins, allowing the tenant to mitigate against a poorly performing store, but providing the developer/landlord the ability to make up the lower base rent threshold through added percentage rent.

Pre-Leasing

Lenders typically require that at least 50–60% of the space be preleased (under actual leases and not just letters of intent), or at least that the major anchor retail tenant be under a signed lease, before closing the construction loan, and will closely review the credit ratings of the tenants. During the pre-leasing process, which may extend into many months, the developer should build an adequate buffer into the required start of construction date in the executed leases, after which the tenant can terminate the lease. The term sheet with the chosen construction lender will also need to allow sufficient time for the developer to reach the target pre-leasing threshold, including the back-and-forth negotiations that occur with retail letters of intent and lease agreements.

Parking, Shared Ride Drop Off, Drive-Through and Contactless Delivery

Most major cities require extensive parking spaces per retail square footage, with a heightened parking requirement for restaurants, typically ranging from 3–5 parking spaces per 1,000 square feet for general retail and 8–10 parking spaces per 1,000 square feet for restaurants. A recent retail development trend is to create regional parking fields with only minor head-in or angle in parking in front of the stores, providing customers with a more walkable environment along the length of the various storefronts. Local zoning codes should be consulted for the actual parking required. As ride-sharing has become more prevalent, project planning should include consideration of adequate off-street or on-street queuing for restaurant and bar customers arriving and departing by Uber or Lyft. If a drive-through restaurant is included in the project the drive-through lane must be carefully located away from parking spaces to avoid trapping parked vehicles that can't depart due to the line of drive-through cars. With food curbside pick-up being more prevalent, short-term parking spaces should be set aside to facilitate this new trend.

Bay Depths

At the outset of planning a retail project the tenant mix is unknown, making design of the various tenants spaces uncertain, particularly determining which parts of the retail center will be sit down restaurants and larger format retailer space that require greater depth. Most retail strip centers locate dine-in uses on the ends, where greater depth is needed, with general retail and more quick dining (e.g., submarine sandwich shops and other fast food, non-drive in concepts) located along the inline space. Bay depths for retail depend largely on the type of tenant, as follows:

Tenant	Depth to Storefront Ratio
Grocery store	2.0 to1.0
Other big box (e.g., pet store, hobby store)	1.5 to1.0
Service tenants (e.g., hair or nail salons)	1.0 to 1.0
Smaller general merchandise, quick dining	Maximum 65 foot depth

Ground Floor Retail in a Vertical Mixed-Use Project

For sake of clarity, one of the discussions above regarding vertical mixed-use projects bears repeating. Ground floor bar and restaurant spaces with outdoor patios can result in higher noise levels, of particular concern when residential units are located on upper floors. Although higher than normal noise levels should be part of urban high rise living, and these people gathering spaces are part of the buzz and excitement of mixed-use projects, attention should be paid to creating a standard for acceptable noise levels and times. In addition, restaurant grease scrubbers and kitchen ventilation should be carefully placed to reduce odors migrating into adjacent retail space or residential units. In larger mixed-use projects, with multiple apartment developers and ground floor retail below each use, consider having all of the ground floor retail owned and controlled by one retail developer (through condominiumization of the retail apart from the apartments), in order to allow the retail owner to effectively manage the tenant mix, as discussed below.

Compatible Tenant Mix

A retail center full of quick dining concepts does not allow for cross-selling among the various tenants on any single visit by a customer. Similarly, a retail center without restaurants eliminates longer-term, more relaxed visits to the center. A balanced retail center creates more opportunities for customers to interact with the development, and will enhance the revenue of the tenants and, through percentage rent, the developer. In larger retail centers, the developer should "curate" the tenants like art—providing customers a wide-variety of national and local shops and restaurants to provide a true shopping and dining experience. Savvy retail developers are using artificial intelligence software to pre-tenant a new project with a tenant mix that will optimize demand and cross-selling opportunities for the overall center. As dining out continues to expand in the United States, new community retail centers are trending toward including 8–10 restaurants versus the 2–4 dining options that were included in older centers.

Periodic Remodeling

As retail centers age they can also become tired and out-of-date. Successful centers are remodeled every 10 to 12 years, with upgraded lighting and landscaping, parking and drive aisle repaving, and new facades, signage, security and patios/seating areas.

Important Lease Provisions

Additional critical terms likely to arise in negotiating individual retail leases include:

- **Operating (or "go dark") covenants**: Most leases of retail space require the tenant to operate during certain days and hours, subject to certain rights to close during renovations, inclement weather and over holidays. The landlord includes these provisions so that parts of the retail center are not closed, presenting the center as not successful and limiting the potential for cross-selling from the closed business to the other open establishments.
- **Exclusivity**: Directly competing businesses within a retail center create an issue for both the landlord and the tenant. As discussed above, the landlord should want a diverse tenant mix to draw a broader range of customers to the center, and the tenant will require the right to operate its business without fear of revenue reduction from a competitor. Two nail salons in the same retail center would not be helpful to either the landlord or the tenant. The landlord should expect tenants to raise the need for the exclusive right to run their form of business within the center, while the tenant must be willing to allow the landlord flexibility to allow competing but synergistic uses (e.g., a Chinese restaurant and a taco shop; a nail salon and a hair style salon that provides ancillary manicures).

22 Hotel Development

Hotels are enticing yet unstable real estate investments—a five-star or boutique hotel is high design and high cost, but if successful, high reward. However, in an economic downturn hotels are the first real estate sector to suffer reduced occupancy and operational losses and are highly prone to whiplash from national and international events such as terrorism, economic recessions, pandemics and travel restrictions. As the economy improves they are the last sector to return slowly back to profitability. Due in large part to this volatility, of all the real estate genres, hotel developments are the most difficult to finance. Finally, due to the extended time to design, structure, finance, construct and open a hotel, the project can begin at a point when hotels are in favor, and complete in the midst of a downturn.

Although a hotel is technically a real estate development, opening a hotel is in many ways more like starting a new entrepreneurial business, with substantial employee overhead and where the customer base turns over every few days. Hotel performance centers around metrics: occupancy, average daily room rate (ADR) and revenue per available room (REVPAR), measured against how the proposed hotel compares to others in its "competitive set" (same quality in the same sub-market). After a site is located, commissioning a market study is the starting point for any hotel development, as a seasoned hotel market analyst can help pinpoint what quality of hotel to develop within that submarket.

Hotel Star Ratings/Categories

Historically, the industry has graded hotels by 1–5 "star levels" awarded by a number of rating agencies and websites, generally described as follows:

- A one-star rating simply means that the hotel offers basic accommodations and limited amenities.
- Although similar to a one-star hotel, a two-star hotel is generally part of a larger chain and offers a few more amenities.
- Three-star hotels are typically part of larger, more upscale chains or hotel groups.

DOI: 10.1201/9781003264514-22

- Four-star hotels are large, upscale establishments, fully staffed, and complete with tons of extras.
- Five-star hotels are the most luxurious in the world.[1]

To create further confusion, other industry experts, such as Smith Travel Research, rank hotels with an entirely different standard, breaking down hotel chains by category based on chain-wide ADR:

- Economy
- Midscale
- Upper Midscale
- Upscale
- Upper Upscale
- Luxury

Finally, the hotel chains market their hospitality offerings with categories that are more easily understandable to the public, using terms like limited service, extended stay and full service.

Choice of Hotel Marque

Working with the market study's suggestions on how to position the proposed hotel within the star ratings or categories, the developer then determines how to brand the hotel, choosing among the various marques held by the well-known hotel branding companies like Marriott (e.g., JW Marriott, St. Regis, Ritz Carlton, Westin, Aloft, Residence Inn), Hilton (e.g., Hilton, Waldorf Astoria, DoubleTree, Embassy Suites Hotels, Hilton Garden Inn, Hampton Hotels, Homewood Suites), or Choice Hotels (e.g., Clarion, EconoLodge, Rodeway Inn, Comfort Inn), Best Western and Intercontinental Hotels Group (Intercontinental, Crowne Plaza, Kimpton, Indigo, Holiday Inn), among others.

Pre-existing or planned hotels in the submarket may have an exclusive right to the desired brand, which can only really be determined based on discussions with the hotel branding company, who will also have input and provide direction as to the appropriate positioning of the proposed hotel within the chain's branding strategy. Each of the hotel branding companies have published "brand standards" for their various hotel marques that are set forth in extensively detailed manuals on required color schemes, amenities, finish quality and services. In one-, two- and three-star hotels, the brand standards are almost construction plans and specifications, outlining design details and materials down to paint colors and precise plumbing fixtures. For upper-level hotels, the brand standards are much more flexible, but also much more amorphous, where the Brand development standards are left to the discretion of the Brand development manager. The hotel developer should secure a thorough understanding of the brand standards and share these requirements with the project architect, interior designer and contractor so that all the project team members are operating off the same playbook.

Alternatively, in and near central office districts, suburban office parks or high-end vacation destinations, the developer may decide to build a boutique, unbranded hotel, free from the fees charged by and the design oversight required by the traditional hospitality companies, hiring a third-party management company that provides concierge level services. While the freedom to design and manage without oversight may at first blush seem appealing, boutique hotels also must operate outside the reservation systems and the brand identity offered by the hotel branding companies, typically relying on the more discerning (and limited quantity of) travelers who value unique experiences over standardized rooms and decor. Boutique hotels tend to be expensive, targeting the luxury consumer, requiring a lengthy period to gain traction and financially stabilize, which explains why boutique hotel development tends to be the playground for multimillionaires and billionaires, many of whom are not primarily in the real estate business.

Hotel Operations

For four-star and up hotels, the hospitality operating company will normally insist on also operating the hotel under a hotel management agreement (HMA). In some cases the hotel branding company may allow a highly respected third party hotel operator; however, in this case the combined fees charged by the branding company and by the third party operator will likely be higher than the fees that would be charged if the branding company were also operating the hotel. For three-star and below hotels/motels, the branding company will normally allow third party management, subject to pre-approval of the management company.

Ancillary Uses

In broad strokes, with four-star and up hotel projects, the hotel branding company will want input into and approval of almost every aspect of the project, including any ancillary uses—a third party restaurant or retail on the ground floor, a parking garage used by the public or adjacent properties; branded condominium residences; etc. In this case, the hotel branding company will require approval over the selection of retail tenants and restaurants to determine how they "fit" with the brand, and if condominiums that share the hotel marque are developed adjacent to the hotel (e.g., Ritz Carlton Residences next to a Ritz Carlton Hotel), the hotel branding company will have design approval over the condo building, will review the condo sale materials and will have approval over shared services and the condo management company. Because parking is critical to hotels (although less so in the era of Uber and Lyft), the parking facilities are likely to be managed by the hotel branding company. The hotel branding company will also manage and charge a fee for overseeing these third-party operations.

Term of Hotel Management Agreement

Hotel brand management agreements (HMAs) tend to have long terms, such as 20 years with at least one 10-year extension. The HMA will include an early termination clause if certain performance metrics are not met, such as the failure to attain at least 90% of budgeted net operating income and 80% of REVPAR for two consecutive quarters. HMAs are not terminable on sale, except with a termination fee that is either a fixed amount or a multiple of the prior year's fees paid to the hotel branding company.

Fees

HMAs provide for a variety of fees payable to the manager, with the base fee payable as a percentage of gross income (averaging in the 3–4% range and including the net income from third party operations within the hotel such as retail or restaurants), an incentive fee based on exceeding net operating income targets (averaging 1% of excess gross income), technical service fees, design review fees, reservation system fees and brand marketing fees.

Owner Input into Management

In the United States, the hotel staff are employed by the management company (although their salaries and benefits are reimbursed by the hotel owner), whereas outside the US the hotel staff are typically employed by the hotel owner with the hotel branding company or management company appointing certain key personnel. The HMA between the owner and either the hotel branding company or third-party management company should provide certain basic rights to the owner, including approval rights over key personnel (general manager, controller and director of marketing and sales), approval over the operating budget, delivery of monthly hotel operating statements and periodic meetings to discuss operational issues.

Preparing for Hotel Opening and the Construction Contract

As previously mentioned, in many ways hotels are less pure real estate and more an operating business, with a large 24/7 staff. The hotel management company will need 3–4 months to hire and train the employees. In addition, the management company will begin to take room, conference, wedding and other reservations months in advance of opening. The construction contract should clearly outline timing for finishing the ground floor lobby, common areas, conference rooms or ballrooms and guest room blocks, and the contractor should keep the owner and management company updated on construction status and notify the owner and the management company months in advance of hotel construction completion. Failure to open on time can result in significant costs to the owner, including an immediate impact on the hotel's reputation. The construction contract should provide substantial penalties for the contractor's failure to provide adequate advance notice of the opening date and for failure to meet completion deadlines.

Note

1 www.investopedia.com/financial-edge/0410/navigating-the-hotel-star-system.aspx

23 Office Development

Similar to retail projects, preleasing and construction timing are also critical to the success of large urban office developments. Lenders typically require 50–60% of the office space be under signed leases before construction can commence. Planning for an office project often begins with negotiations with a large, well-known lead tenant such as a law firm, accounting firm, insurance company or financial institution.

Locating a Lead Tenant

Many of the large commercial real estate brokerage firms have divisions that act as office leasing agents for either landlords or tenants, and track upcoming lease expirations, such that one of the first steps for the developer is to engage an agent to scour their database and reach out to brokers representing tenants seeking new office space for potential lead tenants.

Lead Tenant Negotiations

Prospective lead tenants are in a superior negotiating position and can demand very favorable lease terms, such as reduced rent, renewal periods with capped increases in rent, additional free parking, higher tenant finish-out allowances and other concessions. Larger tenants are often in dialogue with several office developers, pitting them against each another in the bidding process, as users of large blocks of office space with expiring leases tend to be a limited commodity at any one point in time. The first office developer to land a large tenant will be the first to build, capturing a large share of the office tenants currently in the market and foreclosing out other competing developments.

Office Lease Letters of Intent

A well-drafted office lease letter of intent covers the following basic terms:

- **Non-binding:** The LOI should start and end with a statement that it is non-binding and is not a contract, which will only arise with execution of the

DOI: 10.1201/9781003264514-23

formal lease. LOIs normally provide for termination exercisable by either party if the lease is not executed within a certain timeframe.

- **Approximate square footage of space to be leased**: The parties should agree on the location of the leased space, and the approximate square footage of the leased space. The actual size of the space will be determined by later measurement after the space is built out. The LOI should also describe the common area factor applied to the leased space area to determine the gross leased area.
- **Term and renewal periods**: Most office leases in newly constructed buildings have longer terms, ranging from 5–10 years or more, and allow the tenant to renew the lease for specified periods of time, although rent may increase in the renewal period to the then-current market rate for similar space.
- **Rent**: The calculation of rent payments, any up-front free rent and rent increases over time (including renewal periods) should all be clearly stated, often in table format.
- **Tenant improvement (TI) allowance**: The amount of TI allowance granted to a tenant is directly related to the size of the tenant and whether the developer needs this tenant as the lead tenant, the annual rent paid and the term of the lease. The owner/developer needs a longer term and higher rent to amortize larger TI allowances over the life of the lease.
- **Parking**: The LOI should state whether any free parking comes with the lease, the location of the parking, whether reserved or unreserved, and any parking charges. Most larger leases allow for a set number of free parking spots, with a smaller number of spots reserved for executives.
- **Common area maintenance (CAM) charges**: The LOI should clarify the responsibility of the tenant to pay for common area charges such as taxes, insurance, landscaping, heating and air conditioning of the common areas, etc.
- **Signage**: Landlord and tenant should agree on the size and location of any tenant signage on the building, and who is responsible for securing signage permits. In most cities the amount of signage allowed on an office building is limited and signage is only given to a few key tenants.
- **Building completion deadlines and termination rights**: Most major tenants are vacating their current lease and moving to the new building, with a fixed date by which they must exit their current premises or face "holdover rent" that is often 1.5× or 2.0× of their normal rent. In addition, failure of the new building to complete on time will cause disruption to the tenant's employees, who may be forced to find alternative temporary workspace. The LOI should outline the tenant's remedies for late delivery, which may include termination of the lease and the payment of liquidated damages to the tenant. On the owner/landlord's side, the project general contractor should face substantial liquidated damages for late delivery given the consequential damages incurred by the owner for delayed construction completion.

24 Seniors' Developments

As the baby boomer generation continues to age and with average life expectancy now being 79 years of age, seniors will make up an expanding percentage of the US population (increasing from 13% of the population being 65 years of age or older in 1990 to an anticipated 22% in this age range in 2030), making development of age-restricted seniors' housing a reliable growth industry for the foreseeable future.

Unlike other real estate genres, housing and caring for seniors has largely fallen to smaller local nonprofit and for-profit developers due to the relatively small size (150 units or less) of most seniors' housing projects.

Types of Seniors' Projects

The seniors' housing market has subdivided along level of care needs, into four basic categories:

- **Independent living** (IL) for "active adults" who have a second home in another city or no longer desire to own and maintain a home, but are still capable of handling all of their daily basic needs. Although the typical age in IL housing is under 70, those capable of living independently may be in their eighties. IL housing may be zero lot line patio homes, duplexes or smaller apartment units but with full kitchens. Common areas are designed into the property to facilitate socialization, and if the IL units are part of a seniors' campus, the active adults may still have access to the services offered by the community. IL units are financeable by HUD, whereas seniors' housing projects that contain large commercial kitchens are not eligible for HUD guaranteed loans. Typical amenities include theaters, activity centers and gyms.
- **Assisted living** (AL) communities for seniors who can still live independently, but need assistance with three or more activities for daily living such as taking medicine, bathing or moving about.[1] The property will have microwave only kitchens without ovens or stoves, and meal plans will be offered in common dining facilities. Most AL properties also have activity directors

DOI: 10.1201/9781003264514-24

and extensive organized social events. Given the level of staffing required, most AL properties are limited to less than 120 units.

- **Memory care facilities** for Alzheimer's and dementia patients are often a segregated part of an AL community, offering a greater level of service based on the needs of this population. Although some states allow 1-story construction for memory care units, most states require that these units be non-combustible light-gauge steel.
- **Short-term rehab facilities** are becoming more popular for seniors who have recently undergone surgery or experienced an injury and need temporary services while engaging in physical rehabilitation to regain strength and mobility.
- **Skilled nursing facilities** are really operating medical businesses with doctors, nurses and medical gas that also serve as housing units for those who are in need of constant medical care, either to recover from an ailment or accident before moving back to an AL community, or toward the end of life. Skilled nursing facilities rely heavily on payments from Medicare and Medicaid.

Some developers have created large "life care" or "continuum of care" campuses, where seniors can migrate between housing types based on their need for assistance as they age, and where a couple with one spouse having greater limitations can live within the same community as the other spouse who is capable of independent living.

Debt financing for seniors products can approach 75% loan-to-cost, with a DSCR between 1.25:1.00 and 1.40:1.00, with a guaranty of at least 10% of the loan during positive lending environments, although these guarantees have recently has grown to 25% due to the impact of the COVID-19 pandemic on seniors' facilities.

Simply stated, the factors for determining the most suitable location for a seniors' housing project bifurcate between independent living housing and seniors' housing where a level of care is needed. For the most part IL housing, where the senior is likely to still be driving (or in more recent times, may be capable of using UBER or LYFT for transportation needs), needs to be located near where high concentrations of people between the ages of 55 and 70 currently live, as they will not want to stray far from friends, family, churches or other familiar surroundings. Housing with care (AL, skilled nursing and memory care), on the other hand, should be located near where the population is predominantly people 40–60 years of age, as grown children in this age range are the caregivers for their aging homebound parents. Grown children in this age range still have active lives of their own and may still have their children at home, and having their aging parents located within a short driving distance reduces the stress on those who may be caring for both an older and a younger generation.

Beyond age demographics, for IL projects financial considerations quickly come into play. Ability to pay rent is largely determined by asset levels of seniors within the target market, as most seniors capable of independent living are largely living off of the earnings from their assets, which may include the equity in a house to be sold, along with using 4%-5% of their savings on an annual basis. Census and other data can be mined to determine if the proposed project location is an area where seniors have sufficient net worth. Due to the high level of professional care required in AL, memory care and nursing home facilities, monthly payments are much higher, and grown children are often assisting their parents with these obligations, such that these senior care units are mostly located near higher income, higher home value submarkets.

After a prospective site is chosen, the developer should also thoroughly investigate both existing and proposed competitive seniors' properties to determine occupancy levels, rent amounts and charges for various services.

To differentiate from other properties, seniors' developers often associate the property with a local nonprofit or religious group, who can assist in providing services, transportation, fellowship and prospective tenants.

Entrance Fee Projects vs. Monthly Rental Projects

Independent living and assisted living facilities can be financed using two very different structures. The first is a typical rental model with private equity and debt financing, similar to standard apartment development financing, where no pre-leasing is required prior to securing the construction loan and commencing construction. Alternatively, the developer may require deposits from prospective residents, with a contractual commitment to pay a full, substantial entrance fee (often up to $1 million). These contractual commitments are then pledged to a financial institution, which makes a loan against the total balance of the committed entrance fees, which is then used as the equity for the project and is paired with construction financing. In addition to the entrance fee, the tenant also pays a monthly amount for common areas and services. The entrance fee model is commonly used by not-for-profit seniors' development companies, where the debt may be secured by issuing tax-exempt bonds at a lower interest rate. The vast majority of the entrance fee is typically refundable upon a resident leaving the facility due to death or needing a higher level of care, although sometimes contingent on the owner reselling the unit to another tenant. In some respects entrance fee seniors' projects operate like for-sale condominium properties, as both of these real estate types require substantial pre-sales/commitments before a construction loan and equity will commit to the project.

Staffing Levels and Licensing

As the level of care services increases from assisted living to memory care to skilled nursing, employee counts rise substantially, and unlike most other forms of real estate (except hotels) the staff function more as service providers than property managers. IL projects are not regulated as no medical care is provided, AL and memory care units are subject to state regulation, with skilled nursing being federally regulated due to reliance on payments from Medicare and

Medicaid. Legal counsel should be engaged to review the proposed project to determine the proper license to secure based on the scope of medical services offered.

Marketing, Lease-Up, Operations and Financing

For assisted living, memory care and skilled nursing projects, the vast majority of developers do not self manage, choosing instead to hire third-party management companies with extensive experience in leasing-up seniors' properties and providing senior services. Seniors' properties are marketing and management intensive. Most prospective tenants will be evaluating a number of potential properties, will tour each property multiple times looking at a number of floor plans and service packages, by themselves or with a friend or family member, before making a decision, and if they currently own a home, the house may need to be sold before they can make the move to a seniors' property. When this process is repeated over a hundred residents, the lease-up/ absorption period may be extensive, and having a great marketing team in place months before operations begin is critical, particularly for projects with a large number of units. The professional management company becomes the face of the property, interacting daily with every resident, and their ability to consistently provide the level of service expected by the tenants is critical to the success of the project.

To prospective lenders and equity partners evaluating investing in a seniors' project, the track record, the experience and reputation of the marketing/ management team may be of equal importance with the expertise and financial strength of the developer, such that the management company should be selected early in the development cycle.

Note

1 For a concise checklist of the 12 activities considered in determining whether a senior can live independently, see www.payingforseniorcare.com/activities-of-daily-living.

Appendix 1 Reading Recommendations

Shopping Center Development, by Michael D. Beyard and W. Paul O'Mara
How Real Estate Developers Think: Design, Profits and Community, by Peter Hendlee Brown
Architects of Community, by Torti Gallas + Partners
Cities for People, by Jan Gehl
The Death and Life of American Cities, by Jane Jacobs
Retail Development, by Anita Kramer
Housing for Seniors: Developing Successful Projects, by Douglas R. Porter
Real Estate Development: Principles and Process, by Marc A. Weiss, Gayle A. Berens and Mike E. Miles
Born to Build, narrated by Herb Weitzman and written by Donna Arp Weitzman

Appendix 2 Glossary of Critical Terms

Affidavit of commencement	A notarized document putting the contractor, all laborers and materialmen on notice of the date of project commencement, filed in the public records to establish when construction liens are effective.
As-built survey	As the project nears substantial completion, a survey showing the actual locations of buildings, sidewalks, easements and other on-the-ground conditions, all of which should be within the site boundaries and city set-backs or in appropriate easements.
Basis concerns	The focus of equity investors on the impact of rising construction costs and land costs, causing the end cost of a project to exceed sales cost per square foot of similar product.
Bonding over	A financial surety bond secured by a contractor to insure over liens filed against the project.
Cap rate	Cash flow before debt service divided by the value of the property. Cap rate is used to determine the value of a project by dividing the annual cash flow by the cap rate.
Certificate of substantial completion	A certificate from the architect on AIA Form G704 that the project has been substantially completed. The certificate of substantial completion is typically required by construction lenders to fulfill a loan covenant that completion occur within a set time frame and by equity partners prior to one of the last payments of the developer fee.
Completion guaranty	An agreement from the developer (or its principals) of all of the loan agreement provisions relating to lien-free completion of the project.
Condominium regime	The documentation used to subdivide real estate into condominium units, share in operational costs and establish a condominium association and condo board to maintain and make decisions regarding common areas.

Construction drawings (CDs)	Construction drawings contain all the details necessary to actually build the project, including a full set of specifications—listing specific material, supply and equipment providers and manufacturers.
Contingency	Line items in the project budget that are not allocated to specific costs, but are available for cost overruns under certain conditions set forth in the construction loan agreement.
Contribution agreement	A contract with the developer where the landowner contributes land to the development joint venture in exchange for an ownership stake in the joint venture.
Cost overrun	The excess of actual development costs over the agreed-upon development budget.
Crystallization	Post-completion of the project, the ability of the developer to establish a fixed percentage entitlement to distributions, eliminating the distribution waterfall.
Dead deal costs	Project pursuit costs that are not recoverable when a project does not ultimately commence construction.
Debt service coverage ratio (DSCR)	The ratio of cash flow before debt service to the debt service payment, typically measured on an annual basis.
Debt yield	The ratio of the project net operating income to the loan amount.
Design drawings (DDs)	The next phase of design drawings, after schematics, where the drawings are more detailed, laying out the entire interior of the project, including details like mechanical, electrical and plumbing (MEP) layouts; cabinet locations; office and amenities; elevator cores and stairwells; etc.
Down date endorsement	A certification from the title company that no liens have been filed against the project since the date of the prior draw request.
Draw request	The accounting from the contractor to the owner of all construction activities during the prior month, along with required lien releases. The owner then submits its own draw request to the construction lender and equity partner, adding in consultant and other soft costs directly incurred by the owner.
Due diligence (DD) period	The timeframe in a purchase and sale agreement (PSA) when the developer's earnest money is refundable and during which the developer and its consultants determine if the site is suitable for the project. May also be called the *feasibility period* or the *inspection period*.

Environmental or hazardous materials indemnity	An agreement from the developer (or its principals) to indemnify the lender against any liability the lender may incur by reason of any adverse environmental conditions on the property.
Equity multiple	The multiple determined by amount of cash returned from making a project equity investment divided by the amount of the equity investment.
Feasibility period	See *Due diligence period*.
Financing package	The "pitch book" used by the developer to attract equity partners, outlining the project details, location and proforma financial performance
Force majeure	Events beyond the control of the developer, such as hidden soil conditions, environmental conditions and supply disruptions.
Forced sale or buy-sell	If the LP Partner will not allow crystallization, the right of the developer to force the LP Partner to purchase the developer's interest in the project, normally at a price determined by the developer's amount of distributable cash if the project were sold at fair market value.
GP partner	Typically a family office, wealthy individual or foreign office that funds a portion of what would otherwise be the developer's equity, and that may also help fund project predevelopment costs or developer overhead.
Ground lease	A contract where the landowner enters into a long-term lease of land to the development venture in lieu of selling the site.
Guaranteed maximum price (GMP) contract	A construction contract that provides for the contractor to be paid the cost of construction plus overhead and a set percentage in contractor profit, but subject to a maximum price.
Inspection period	See *Due diligence period*.
Issued for construction plans (IFCs)	After the architect and developer have responded to all of the city comments, the architect will issue the IFC plans, a final set of plans that are the playbook by which the general contractor builds the project.
Letter of intent (LOI)	A nonbinding summary of terms between parties that is used as an outline for drafting a binding contract.
Leverage	The use of debt and equity from limited partners and co-general partners to increase the return on the developer's equity.
Lien releases	As part of the draw request, the developer secures "conditional lien releases" from the contractor and all subcontractors and materialmen, releasing any liens against the property for the current month's work, but subject to receiving payment for such work, along with "unconditional lien releases," releasing any liens for prior months (for which payment has already been made).

Loan balancing	A loan agreement provision requiring the equity partners to contribute additional funds if project costs exceed the remaining construction loan funds and the previously agreed to equity contributions.
Loan to cost (LTC)	The ratio of loan amount divided by the total development cost of the project.
Loan to value (LTV)	The ratio determined by dividing the construction loan amount by the as-built stabilized fair market value of the project.
LP partner	The developer's joint venture partner that provides the majority of the development equity.
Nondisturbance and attornment agreement (NDA)	A side letter agreement between various parties providing financing for a project, where those holding superior lien rights agree to provide inferior lien holders with notice and opportunity to cure defaults by the project owner.
Nonrecourse carveout guaranty	An agreement from the developer (or its principals) agreeing to indemnify the lender from any cost or expense incurred by reason of the bad acts of the borrower or its principals.
Notice to proceed	A letter from the project owner to the contractor stating that construction can commence.
OPM	"Other's people's money"—a pejorative shorthand for using third party funds to increase leverage and the developer's rate of return.
Option to ground lease	An agreement by a landowner to enter into a Ground Lease.
Owner–architect agreement (OA)	The contract between the owner and the architect for designing the project.
Permit set of plans	The fully detailed set of architectural and engineering plans submitted to the city as part of the construction permitting process.
Platting or replatting	The city or county process of subdividing a larger tract of land into multiple land tracts, with particular focus on providing access and utilities to all of the resulting tracts.
Proforma	A multi-tabbed financial spreadsheet detailing project costs, financing and annual income and expense, and outlining the important project performance metrics for lenders and equity partners.
Promote	The portion of the developer's return from the project that is in excess of the amount the developer would receive based only on the percentage of capital contributed by the developer.
Purchase and Sale Agreement (PSA)	The contract between a landowner and the developer for the acquisition of a project site.

Pursuit costs	Costs incurred by the developer in locating a site, performing site due diligence, engaging consultants, preparing architectural plans and otherwise pursuing a project.
Schematic design drawings (SDs)	Initial architectural drawings laying out the basics of the core and exterior of the project, without delving into interior design.
Subordination	An agreement by one party holding a superior lien position against real estate to place it lien rights behind the lien position of a party holding a lower lien priority position.
Sweat Equity	The developer's time, energy and focus applied to the project.
Syndication	A group of investors that may fund a portion of what would otherwise be the developer's equity.
Tenant improvement (TI) allowance	A set amount of funds provided by a landlord to a tenant to finish out the tenant's leased space.
Value engineering	A pejorative term for lowering the cost of a project by reducing amenities, picking lower cost materials, and possibly redrawing the project.
Waterfall	The enumerated tiers of cash flow, sale proceeds or operating cash flow distributions between equity partners.

Index